D1613849

Tony's: the cookbook

THE COOKBOOK

by George Fuermann
with recipes by Tony Vallone

SHEARER PUBLISHING/*Fredericksburg*

EDITOR: Jean Evans Hardy
PHOTOGRAPHER: Bill Stites
ILLUSTRATOR: Kenneth G. Boehnert
FOOD STYLIST: Kathryn George

First published in the United States in 1986 by
Shearer Publishing
406 Post Oak Road
Fredericksburg, Texas 78624

Library of Congress Cataloging in Publication Data
Fuermann, George, 1918–
Tony's : the cookbook.

Recipes by Tony Vallone.
Includes index.
1. Cookery, Italian. 2. Cookery. 3. Tony's (Restaurant : Houston, Tex.) I. Vallone, Tony. II. Tony's (Restaurant : Houston, Tex.) III. Title.
TX723.F8 1986 641.5945 86-20382

ISBN 0-940672-38-3

Manufactured in the United States of America
SECOND PRINTING

The publisher gratefully acknowledges the material assistance provided in this project by Gump's and Tiffany's, both of Houston.

For
Maria Aiello Vallone,
Ciro Aiello,
and
Mary Vallone Patronella

TONY VALLONE *extends special thanks to friend and associate* TINO ESCOBEDO *for his patience and expertise in tasting, and to his wife,* DONNA AQUILINA VALLONE, *for her inspiration and encouragement.*

Contents

Preface

There is no love sincerer
than the love of food.
GEORGE BERNARD SHAW

I AM A DINER, not a cook. I have made chili a few times, the kind that comes with all the dry ingredients measured into little packets. I have made a tuna fish salad a few times, too, but the only cooking involved was making a couple of hard-boiled eggs. On the other hand, I have more than six decades of training as a diner. No matter. Tony Vallone, a magnificent and an inspired cook, prefers cooking *and* dining to most other human activities.

Do I live to eat rather than eat to live? I do. I prefer the words "dine" and "dining" to "eat" and "eating." The first two words have character; they describe what is in my mind when I go to table or anticipate doing so. The verb "dine," in my personal lexicon, means good food and good wine and good companions and good talk and good health. Dining is the only art that does not need to be practiced.

This book is a culinary docent for diners, and above all for cooks. Of course, the diner must be granted some say in cooking. He or she is the end of cooking, its object. Though the cook's role is far greater, it is not everything. The cook is the giver, no matter who pays for the food; the diner receives. Eating, W.H. Auden wrote, is a "pure act of taking." It is done entirely for ourselves, the first of our necessities.

Mine is the view of the hedonist, though some would call it the view of the shiftless, for cooking is work even to those who love to cook. That may be the cause of cooking's pedestrian cast in many minds. To speak of making love or of making money is understood as an aspiration worthy of achievement. As a rule, though, to speak of cooking raises the level of thought only a little above the level of house cleaning or doing the laundry.

That will hardly be the case with this book's readers. Jean-François Revel, in his remarkable book *Culture and Cuisine*, speaks of the "dialogue between the food-lover and the creator that allows the former to find an interpreter capable of realizing his ambitions and the latter to give free reign to his imagination, knowing that its labors will be understood." Revel was writing of a seventeenth-century French nobleman and his chef, but the point is still valid, especially so in the rapport between Tony Vallone and his diners. Tony deals with gastronomy in the sense Brillat-Savarin meant when he called gastronomy "the intelligent knowledge of whatever concerns man's nourishment."

The restaurant's motto, The Poetry of Dining, is fitting. After all, most Italians are poets, and it was the Italians who led the French to *haute cuisine*. As Rudolph Chelminski noted in writing about *la cuisine française*, "The French owe much to the Italians, that admirable people of precursors, in the field of culinary expertise." That debt began when the fourteen-year-old Catherine de Medici, a Florentine princess, crossed the Alps to marry the man who would become Henry II. She brought with her to sixteenth-century France her own Florentine cooks—the genesis of French culinary art.

This is not a book to read all at once, but one to be taken, like the great dinners served in Tony's wine cellar, a course at a time, leaving time in between courses. A good dinner ought to be a celebration, a small ecstasy, a sort of petite holiday, hundreds of which, each different from every other, may be formed in the pages ahead. The back of Tony's menu notes an Italian proverb that should apply to this book as well: "One does not age at the table." The front of the menu contains a Friedrich von Hardenberg quotation that is the essence of the restaurant's spirit: "Dinnertime is the most wonderful period of the day and perhaps its goal . . . the blossoming of the day."

"A good book about food informs us of matters with which we are to be concerned all our lives," Clifton Fadiman wrote. "Sight and hearing lose their edge, the muscles soften, even the most gallant of our glands at last surrenders. But the palate may persist in glory almost to the very end."

"This is a personal book," Tony said one day when he, our editor, Jean Hardy, and I were planning various sections of the recipes. "It's a book of food that interests me personally as much as it is of food that concerns me professionally."

Many of these recipes are easy to prepare; some are more complicated and take a lot of time. All require the cook's interest and attention, but as Tony has said, and as he practices to a fare-thee-well, "No recipe, except one that is absolutely basic, should be taken as unalterable." Try it as given. If it suits, fine. If not, alter it. As someone once said, "Every recipe is waiting expectantly to be improved upon." Tony has said of recipes generally, "A dish must look good and sound good, but above all it must taste good, and often what sounds wonderful on paper will disappoint when you taste it."

Every recipe in this book is tested, and many retested, in the restaurant's kitchen. Moreover, and one more reason we were lucky to have her as our editor, a fair number of these dishes were made at home by Jean for her family, in some cases if she questioned anything, in others if she was just curious about a dish. She is an inspired home cook, which, of course, is the person to whom these recipes are addressed.

. . . Dewey, Boehnert, Crispin.

Kenneth G. Boehnert, Andre A. Crispin and Richard A. Dewey were asked to consult with us on the wine recommendations that accompany many recipes. They are three sound, unpretentious and lifelong wine advocates. What came forth are mostly moderate to low-priced wines; anyone who can pay for a Le Montrachet or a Chateau Latour does not need a guide.

These wine recommendations are but modest proposals. Should you have decided upon, say, the Redfish with Oysters (page 147) for dinner, and you wonder a little what wine might suit it, give the suggested wine a whirl. This trio of vinous savants, not to mention Tony, turned an abrupt thumbs-down on my feeling that any good wine goes well with any kind of food.

I have already mentioned Jean Hardy, the editor of this book. She was our disciplinarian, but above all she was our benediction. She caused the book to cohere through her extraordinary intelligence and her estimable common sense.

Tony and Ruth Owens and I have been friends—and often disputants about table matters—for more than twenty years. The book's staff, as it were, consisted of Tony and six aides: Ruth and I; Jean Hardy and Donna Vallone, Tony's wife; and those two gifted men, the artist Ken Boehnert and the photographer Bill Stites. Epicurus told us long, long ago to find an agreeable use for our faculties in "the intelligent enjoyment of the pleasures of the table." That is this book's motto.

We wish our readers as much pleasure in using this book as we have had in getting it all together. Tony and I say, with Fritz Brenner, that superlative chef in Rex Stout's Nero Wolfe stories: "I do not think that this book [*The Nero Wolfe Cookbook*, by Rex Stout] will make your food any worse. At least it should help with some of the facts."

G.M.F.

Introduction

The warm glow of a good meal
or a bottle of wine . . . may be temporary,
but then so is life.
MICHAEL KORDA

HOUSTON WAS SLOW to win a reputation for good dining. In 1871, speaking at the Houston Fair Grounds long after he had advised young men to go West, Horace Greeley offered more advice: Texas, he said, "is in urgent need of . . . fifty thousand cooks." What occasioned this belittling remark remains a mystery, for nowhere in America in the 1870s, except perhaps in the cities of the Eastern seaboard, was the cuisine *haute* or even, one supposes, bourgeois. It was practical.

Houston did at length develop the convention of good public dining, chiefly from the 1890s to the time of World War I. The old Sauter Restaurant and the alfresco dining room of the Brazos Hotel, among others, to judge from menus and contemporary reports, offered dining rather than eating in the 1890s. At the same time, the Grand Central Hotel Dining Hall, at 713 Washington Avenue, served ten-course dinners for fifty cents; entrees included suckling pig, larded quail and green goose served with calf's foot jelly; desserts included English plum pudding and fresh strawberries.

Even earlier, in 1883, the Ladies' Association of Houston's First Presbyterian Church published *The Texas Cook Book*, whose subtitle is *A Thorough Treatise on the Art of Cookery*. The 186-page book, the first cookbook to be published in Texas, is a remarkable work; more than a century later it can still be used to fulfill its original mission and for the pleasure given by its astonishing vitality. A good omelet—very hard to find, especially in restaurants—is one of the little miracles of dining. Judge *The Texas Cook Book* from the down-to-earth intelligence of this recipe:

> An Omelet. It is an easy thing to do, and not often well done. The trouble lies in the fact that most cooks overbeat their eggs. A simple omelet is not a souffle. Break all the eggs into one plate, *stir* rather than *beat* them, and to each three eggs, put in *one* teaspoon cold water. I do not like milk. Salt and pepper the eggs moderately (American cooks use too much pepper), take some parsley and chop it. Let the parsley be fine—fine (American cooks never chop parsley fine enough), put two ounces of sweet butter in your pan—lard for an omelet is an abomination. When the butter is *very* hot, pour in the eggs; the instant that it is cooked on one side (*not crisp*, but simply *cooked*), turn it quickly and cook the other side. Double it over when you serve it, on a very hot plate. The cold water used makes the omelet light and moist.

No question that Houston had "instructed cooks" by the 1880s. Like most of the rest of the nation, though, Houston had little chance to show culinary promise during the successive debacles of Prohibition and the Great Depression. Then, after World War II, came the era—to Houston, especially, but also to Texas—identified by the phrase "Land of the Big Rich." This gaudy period, by no means without its stimulants, made any elevation of cookery beyond sirloin steak, barbecue and fried catfish unlikely, though I am not defaming those three great dishes. We ate well, but right after World War II our high cuisine was more likely to be found in homes than in public eating places.

To give some, if an unjust, idea of where Houston stood in this respect, the book *Great Restaurants of America*, published in 1960, included four restaurants in Dallas, but no other in Texas or in all of the American Southwest. The book was written by Ted Patrick, the editor of what was then *Holiday* magazine, and Silas Spitzer, also a New Yorker. It was Houston's burden that the North disapproved of the megalomania of some Houston wildcatters. So did many Houstonians.

But gastronomy was again showing itself in Houston. Henry Barbour had much to do with it. A perfectionist, a taciturn Yankee, a reincarnation of one of the Sun King's princes of gastronomy, Barbour came to Houston to be manager of the Houston Club. He was an early rendition of Tony Vallone. Little by little, he built a stunning wine cellar for the club. Then, to assist in consuming the wines, he organized the Houston chapters of, first, Les Amis d'Escoffier and then the Confrerie de la Chaine des Rotisseurs. Oddly, Barbour was never repelled by the humbug aspects of most wine and food societies, but he possessed every right instinct of the classical gourmand, of the natural hedonist. Some of his dinners were served to nearly two hundred persons, far too many for culinary distinction, yet somehow he made a success of each. I was there. Henry Barbour revealed the benedictions of gastronomy that many had suspected without evidence. To some extent, it owed to Barbour that the Seventh of April Club (1964), the Commanderie de Bordeaux (1966) and many other wine and food groups were organized and have flourished in Houston ever since.

Another who made a difference was a shy and gentle Swiss, an orchid-grower, who came to Houston to be executive chef of the old Rice Hotel, when the Rice still hoped to survive. That was in the 1960s, and the man was Charles Finance. The most nearly serene of chefs in my experience, he prefigured Tony Vallone in stressing the use of the Texas Gulf Coast's regional foods. "As a now cosmopolitan city," he wrote in 1965, "Houston is growing in culinary achievements as fast as any large city in the United States."

There was a troublesome aspect of dining anywhere in Texas that limited any opportunity the state might have had to rival the restaurant centers of most other states: liquor-by-the-drink was illegal in Texas for more than half a century until 1971. Until then, spirits could be served only in private clubs in so-called "wet" counties, which as a rule were the urban counties. The sale of liquor is an important part of a restaurant's profit; without it, gastronomy in Texas had less chance to succeed than it did elsewhere.

And yet, our restaurant culture was growing. No great restaurant, not Tony's or any other, matured without reference to other restaurants and to its region's past. Many Houstonians can still recall with affection Ye Old College Inn, Ernest and Dell Coker's restaurant on South Main Street near the Rice University campus. (Remember the Inn's Dichotomy of Oysters? Two Oysters Casino, two Oysters Bienville, two Oysters Rockefeller and two Oysters something else, as I recall, wishing the dish were before me right now.) And many will recall, wistfully, the Green Parrot, where Vira Fredericks proved for years that plain fare—fried chicken, steaks and a broiled fish dish—could be epicurean, and that Houstonians would drive a long way out of their way to eat them.

And Ernst Kurt's Snack Shop, with its remarkable Hungarian goulash; and Schwartsberg's, close in on Main Street, with what was surely the world's best potato soup; and Hebert's Ritz, now at least half a century old, and its best-of-all remoulade sauce, which some of us asked for as a salad dressing; and Madeline Pollard, who fed cafe society, as we then called an extravagance of egos.

Then there was the pumpkin pie and the rice pudding, but especially the pumpkin pie, at the Rice Hotel Coffee Shop. And across Texas Avenue from the Rice was the oyster bar at Kelley's Steak House, oysters on one side of the partition, steaks on the other, and I wish it were still there. Even more do I yearn to taste again the Oysters Louisiane at La Louisiane Restaurant across from the Shamrock Hilton on South Main Street. Any city that possessed Mike Salvato, as Houston did for many years, could call itself a center of cookery. First his Solari's, in Houston, and then his Mike's Rendezvous, at Algoa, near Alvin, marked long steps toward heightened gastronomy. His French-grilled oysters was a dish so generous in its reward to the palate that any factual description of it would appear to be fantasy.

Nothing has been said of the many other restaurants that knew just what to do with the preeminent foods of the region, led by the harvest of the Gulf of Mexico: red snapper, redfish, flounder, Gulf sea trout, and above all our blue crabs and their lovely, delicate fresh lump meat, and our shrimp and oysters. Indeed, we ate royally, if we wanted to, from whenever it was that we became a city, and certainly we have done so since the late 1940s. Almost without seeming to do so, we developed fine restaurants that lacked only the silver trumpets that proclaimed Manhattan restaurants of the time. We were lucky to have men and women (Helen Corbitt being foremost among the last) who aspired to make dining an experience, to make it theater before that word was applied to wine and food.

I should mention, too, if not in the sense of high cuisine, other foods and other places that many of us longed for—and still do: the Linoleum Club, as the mezzanine was called when the city's Establishment ate there, at James Coney Island when it was not a chain but a single exceptional place on Walker Avenue; and the One's-a-Meal cafes (we didn't know the phrase "fast foods" then), which, in the early 1940s, served a fine filet mignon dinner for seventy-five cents; and the first 2-K Sandwich Shop, at the corner of Main and West Main, and its midnight eggs-in-a-skillet. Barbour and Finance and all the rest, the plain and the grand, each helped form the taste, the appetite for and the longing to share an oasis for epicures—Tony's.

PART ONE

The Restaurant

The Secret Ingredient

If a man be sensible and . . . count at the tips of his
fingers how many things in this life
truly will give him enjoyment, invariably he
will find food is the first one.

LIN YUTANG

SO MANY STORIES are told about Tony's that sorting out the fables and the legends from fact is a little like trying to sort out all the ingredients of a cassoulet after the stew has been cooked. But the stories that *are* true have alone created, layer upon layer, the reality that informs and illumines Tony's. As a critic wrote in 1979, "If a visitor had to choose only one restaurant to dine at in Texas, it would be Tony's." Another wrote in 1982 that the restaurant is "'worth a special journey,' as the *Guide Michelin* would put it." Tony Vallone himself, another critic wrote in 1985, "is simply the tastemaker of Texas."

What gave this cumulative legend a life of its own, aside from Tony Vallone's gifts and inspiration as a restaurateur? Like any mystique, a legend shuns revelation; it cannot be shown by charts or graphs or computer programs. Some say the legend first drew breath the night Lynn Wyatt gave a dinner party for Princess Margaret in the wine cellar—a soiree the princess soon turned, briefly, into a country-western jamboree, with the chamber music violinists fiddling away as at an East Texas hoedown. But no, the legend had matured before then.

Some say the wine list is part of it, and of course it is. After all, wines priced $250 and more a bottle, as on the "Indulgence" section of the wine list at Tony's, are to a legend what *pâté de foie gras* is to an epicure. Though many diners may fail to notice it, others are bewitched by the museum case of rare wines in the entrance hall. Their vintages go back to 1811 and their prices range from $550 to $17,500. But neither the wine list nor the wine museum is more than a slender layer of the legend.

No doubt the legend gained another layer when Luciano Pavarotti twice broke into brief song at a post-opera midnight dinner for sixty given by the Houston Grand Opera Association. ("He is a wonderfully funny man," Tony says of a fellow Italian he much admires.) Tony's, Mimi Swartz wrote in 1979, herself adding a mite to the legend, "is undeniably the most talked-about eating place in the state." Well, yes. Tony serves the hedonist, not to mention the epicure, "who gets nothing better than the cream of everything, but cheerfully makes the best of it," as Oliver Herford described him.

Houston socialite Joanne Davis once described to a T the restaurant's chief accomplishment. People mark the important events of their lives at Tony's, she said. Like Frank Sinatra in his heyday, she added, Tony's is part of everyone's love story. Joanne Davis perceived the essence of the restaurant's success with far more insight than do those who are moved chiefly by what one writer has called the restaurant's "rich, royal and renowned" aspects.

THE SECRET INGREDIENT

A great restaurant is a theater. Each diner is part of the audience. To him or to her, all the other diners are the players. The captains, waiters and other members of the staff are the directors and the stagehands. Restaurants are forums, too—meeting places for talk, romance, business, celebration. Tony has described all this in terms of ballet. "You must be a choreographer to run a restaurant," he says.

From the start, though the scene was modest compared to the Tony's that would come, the restaurant was an oasis. It opened in the spring of 1965 on Sage Road near Westheimer—now part of the Galleria's parking area. Many who never saw the place came to think of it as having been a spaghetti house. It served spaghetti, all right, though even better was the marvelous fettuccine, but it was never a "spaghetti house." The early menus had an Italian bent, but by and large the cuisine was Continental. And the restaurant was popular from the beginning. One writer said of it, many years later, that diners "remember it as a place that was fun to visit, with good food and drink, dancing and one waitress for every four tables. The place was fine with everyone—except Tony."

"It was one waitress for every *six* tables," Tony later recalled. In fact, of course, the true beginning was roughly two decades earlier. Tony Vallone was born in Houston . . . well, few really know when, or are apt to find out. An intensely private person, he yields little of himself, of his plans or aspirations or anything else unless it suits him, which it rarely does. Shy and of an almost apologetic mien in the company of strangers, soft-spoken but well-tempered in will, he reveals those Italian characteristics that we all salute: a rough-and-ready gentleness, warmth, generosity and joy in living.

His mind is supple and sometimes astonishing in its dimension; few who know him could believe that a university education would have been other than an anchor. Of course, the shyness, the withdrawn manner, are little known to friends, nor are these the characteristics that have impressed members of his staff or any of his suppliers. After all, Tony *is* Italian, including in temperament. He speaks Italian so well that Antonio Mastroberardino, one of the foremost Italian winemakers of the twentieth century, said after dining with Tony, "I thought he was born in Italy."

Tony's background in cookery is plain, old-fashioned Italian. The home-cooking that would be his ABC's of cookery was hardly peasant-style, but it was much closer to that than to the luxury and sophistication of the dishes that appear on the restaurant's dinner menus. His first teacher, and the chief culinary influence on his life, was Maria Aiello Vallone, his paternal grandmother. If Tony has forgotten details of his period of kitchen schooling, he has by no means forgotten his love for, or his debt to, Maria Vallone. "She opened my eyes to food," he says. "Growing up, I never knew there was any room but the kitchen."

Maria Vallone cooked for two restaurants and catered, all from her home kitchen. Tony says it follows that she cooked as a professional, not as a home cook. "She was a typical Sorrentina," he says. "She loved to cook fresh seafood and lightly sautéed tomatoes and almost anything containing fresh basil. I watched her make thirty, forty dishes—I can't recall how many now—and my job was to help her. My real job, at least in the beginning, was doing the lifting and mixing—and a lot of the tasting, too."

Maria's younger brother, Ciro Aiello, was also important to Tony. A professor who had once taught anesthesiology in California, he lived part of the year in Sorrento, Italy, and the other part in Houston. Wanting to send Tony to college, this great uncle invited Tony to live with him in Naples to attend the Collegio per Stranieri, a college for foreigners. Ciro died just two months before Tony was to join him in Naples. It would be useless to speculate on Tony's future had he attended the collegio, except to wonder if it would have diverted him from the career he chose. I doubt it.

His grandmother's kitchen, Tony once said, was "a kind of church and marketplace and workshop all in one room." He said she would have been puzzled by, and mocked, such shortcuts as packaged pie crust and precooked rice and TV dinners. "She would have thought them unfit to eat, too," he said. "Simmering an honest Italian sauce or a soup all day long, with the aromas perfuming our house, was not work for her but pleasure. She didn't try to save time; she spent it lavishly for our table. No shortcuts allowed. She used to say, 'Make it right, or don't make it.'"

In some ways he was describing what his restaurant would become. Speaking once of the absence of microwave ovens and of heat lamps and of the other quick-time, fast-food, anti-dining paraphernalia with which most modern restaurants dissemble food, Tony said, as Maria Vallone would have said: "A restaurant kitchen is one place you should not make too modern. Unless you believe, and act upon, the stove-to-table principle, you will be charging your diners high prices for cafeteria food."

Two others who influenced Tony were Edmond M. Foulard and Michael A. Salvato, disparate in every way but each attracted by Tony's promise. Mike Salvato was a warm, remarkable man endowed with practical but inspired culinary gifts. Salvato helped perfect in Tony the hunch, instinct and shading that must cohere to make a great restaurateur. Edmond Foulard, who had been the chef at the old Tony's Restaurant before he started his own award-winning restaurant, was gifted in a more formal, classic way. "Chef Foulard taught me the intricacies of the sauce station," Tony says. Finally, a life-long influence, a wise and loyal adviser, is Tony's aunt, Mary Vallone Patronella, still hale in 1986. She is the Aunt Mary whose name appears in several recipe titles—"A magnificent cook, a truly great baker," Tony says of her. "I used to practice recipes with her. I still get her to sample certain dishes for me," Tony says. "And she can tell me more with a look than others tell me with a thousand words."

It was from his grandmother that Tony picked up another quality that has for years deviled the close friends among his diners. "She was constantly conceiving new ideas for food—maybe a little change to renew interest in a classic, maybe a big change in some other dish to transform it," he says. "She couldn't escape her imagination, fortunately."

Like grandmother, like grandson. Some of Tony's greatest admirers have been known to hope that he will be absent when they go to the restaurant. When he sees friends having dinner at Tony's, though they may have dined to a fare-thee-well, including dessert, out from the kitchen may come a sample of the latest creation, sometimes cooked by Tony himself. "Just taste it, just a bite," he pleads. And of course the friends do—one bite, two, more—and pray that he has not conceived *two* new dishes that week. Though these marvelous adventures never appear on a diner's check, they very soon appear on his or her waistline.

Tony's wife, Donna, says he is "a great saucier and a great seasoner. He mixes his own dry seasonings at home." She does much of the cooking for the family, but Tony cooks as well. "He's an absolute perfectionist," she says. "If it doesn't turn out right, out it goes." One learns from Donna that Tony's perfectionism extends to the feeding of the family dogs. The two mutts are far from being pedigreed specimens, but Tony cannot bring himself to serve them ordinary dog food. Instead, he stir-fries their chow with powdered garlic and other ingredients. "It's good for them," he tells an incredulous observer.

At home or at the restaurant, the rules are the same. "Everything we cook with at home," Donna says, "is fresh. The only canned vegetable in the house is canned tomatoes, the ones Tony imports from Italy for sauces."

Which brings us to one of Tony's chief maxims: No dish can be better than what goes into it. "When you have a widely acclaimed restaurant," Tony has said, "you have an advantage. We pay the highest prices for beef, lamb, veal, poultry and seafood, much of it specially reserved for us. We have first pick of the finest fruits and vegetables. We have specially imported wines and spirits. How can we go wrong with such a head start?"

But he quickly acknowledges that it would be easy to spoil first-class ingredients before they reach the table, to waste the benefit he gets from suppliers who respect him as a discriminating (and difficult) customer. And so at length he has worked out Tony's Ten Commandments for Good Cooking:

I. Cook with gas, never with electricity.

II. Cook with iron, copper or earthenware vessels, never with aluminum.

III. Cook with patience.

IV. Flavor food generously, yet prudently.

V. Taste everything.

VI. Use both hands.

VII. Be neither wasteful nor stingy; be generous without being foolish.

VIII. Let your dishes rest briefly before serving, except sautéed dishes.

IX. Set your table in white, with clear, uncolored glasses and sharp knives.

X. Accent the specialties of the season and especially of your region, serving whatever is best that is available at the moment.

(Privately, Tony has an eleventh commandment: Bury any restaurateur who uses a microwave oven or a heat lamp in the kitchen!)

The savory world of Tony's, of what often strikes me as the restaurant's nutrition for voluptuaries, begins with Tony Vallone's gift for transforming the act of eating into the art of dining, into an experience involving all the senses. This experience may be sublime when Tony is in one of his new-dish phases. A good restaurateur starts with the best materials he can find, and then, as one good chef once said, he spends the rest of his life "learning how not to spoil them." Tony accepts the wry common sense of that, but in fact he is spending the rest of his life learning how to ennoble them.

He thinks of food as an art form, as though he were painting on plates, and on palates. Seeing two friends at table one day, he sent a new appetizer to them and followed it personally. He called it a "side dish" rather than an appetizer, and plainly was as eager for it to please as though he had presented socially one of his children.

"The red [pepper] is for color," he said, adding that it was present first of all for its exquisite taste. "It's a side dish with no name yet—*haricots verts* [green beans] with sunflower seeds and a pinch of bread crumbs, on sweet red pepper."

Tony is nothing if not open-minded, adapting ingredients to his own uses and always exercising his gift for creation, for fantasy. Moreover, as if possessing some sixth sense, he is unbelievably alert to culinary change. Richard Dewey tells the bread pudding story: "Months before bread pudding had any cachet except in cafeterias, Tony was serving this magnificent—at least as he does it—dessert. Months later we were reading about bread pudding in all the food and wine magazines."

Dismayed to serve his celebrated dessert soufflés with a conventional spoon, Tony arranged to have a special soufflé spoon designed (it resembles a flattened soup spoon, but has an indentation like a fish knife). Not liking the conventional fish knife, he designed his own.

It is especially worth noting that Tony's sense of food is by no means confined to the indulgence dishes thought to be at the top of a hedonist's wish list. Diners who happened to be in the restaurant the first winter Thursday that the word "Chili" appeared on the luncheon menu were incredulous. It was as though Cartier (which has given the restaurant its Award of Excellence in Dining) had decided to feature Timex watches. At that time, the price of a bowl of Texas red at Tony's was $9.50.

Once, as a jest, a well-known Houston lawyer ordered chicken-fried steak. Nothing loath, Tony soon served what he briefly thought could be called *Côte de Veau à la Crème*. (By 1985, French had been all but removed from Tony's menus.) Soon it was on the lunch menu, one day a week, as plain Chicken-fried Steak, and now vies with the chili, served on a different day, in popularity. (Both are exceptional of their kind, but I do not go to Tony's to eat chili or chicken-fried steak, no matter how marvelous.) Little by little, dishes of humble origins, the so-called peasant dishes that give food a good name, appeared on the menu at lunch: the Cajun dish Smothered Shrimp over Rice (page 137), turkey with old-fashioned

tony's

CAVIAR

dressing (with an Italian option), chopped steak, Maryland crab cakes. These homely lunch specialties, plain dishes double-daring the menu's haute cuisine, make Tony's, as one diner says, "almost like home"—though his home must be deep in the heart of River Oaks.

But the secret ingredient of this restaurant is its Italian-ness rising unexpected from the classic and traditional cuisines of France and America. What Joseph Wechsberg once wrote, that in Italy "eating is not a serious business as it is in France, where no gourmet would break into song during a meal," informs the joy of Tony's cuisine. "The Latin genius flashes from the kitchen pans," Elizabeth David wrote of Mediterranean cooking, and that is the story of Tony's when all coheres.

THE SECRET INGREDIENT

A Friday luncheon at Tony's, November 1985:

By one o'clock the restaurant is nearly full. The only empty tables are in the bar, where food is not served. The Bordeaux Room holds a large private luncheon; another is being served to some corporation executives in the wine cellar. Directing all this, besides Tony, are Tino Escobedo, the general manager, and Jost Lunstroth, the manager, and the seven captains, aided by the front waiters and the kitchen waiters and the busmen. Altogether, they manage this bounty, this merry total dining fete, with a grace and aplomb that astonish at least one diner, who looks on, at first bemused—and at length with respect.

Two huge dessert soufflés are served to a table of seven Japanese, who have eaten very well for nearly two hours—this as two more dessert soufflés, with the unbelievable height they achieve at Tony's, are served to another table of six. A big block of ice containing a bottle of Stolichnaya Vodka, followed by the sterling-silver crab that always contains fresh Beluga caviar, goes to a table occupied by an obviously contented middle-aged man. He seems to know nearly every woman in the restaurant, and he visits each of them more than once during his long lunch, though his own table is decorated with two women who are much younger than their host.

Whole Poached Salmon, centerpiece for a wine-cellar party

Throughout the room, diners are given a "dessert" that is not on the menu: the bizarre, the flaky, the incredible, the breath-taking fashions—of clothing, to be sure, but also of hair and of faces and of bodies—worn by many of the younger women, and by others who are not so young. "Tony's," a thoroughly reformed ladies' man once said, "is the best people-watching place in the city."

This was lunch, not dinner. No matter when I am to meet someone at Tony's, I go at least half an hour early.

It has been said that Tony is a great saucier. Ironically, the culinary strictures in vogue during his restaurant's ascendancy tended to diminish the art of a gifted saucier—but also, at least in Tony's case, to stimulate creativity. As one of the first restaurateurs in Houston to offer "heart-healthy" dishes, though they were never called that at Tony's, he offered his diners a choice of the spare, so-called lean-cuisine dishes, joining taste and nutrition, but also of the more traditional, classic-style dishes pared of some of their richness.

"A diet-conscious society tries to shun the ingredients that raise food to the epicurean level that many diners insist upon," Tony says. "I cannot cook well without using the finest butter. The secret of good cooking is the finest butter and other ingredients—and patience. I rarely use flour in my sauces, and then minutely; butter and cream, yes. The great cream sauces must have both. You finish off with the butter."

Tony's personal experience has been his teacher. Like many of us, Tony has tried in vain all his adult life to be what he and most who surround him are unlikely ever to be: slender. Those who know him are puzzled by his passion to achieve the unachievable, given everything about him. For one thing, the fifth of his Ten Commandments of Good Cooking is, "Taste everything." For another, a slender Tony would mock the restaurant. One of the great chef-proprietors of the twentieth century, Fernand Point of the Restaurant de la Pyramide, in Vienne, France, once observed: "You've got to love to eat well if you want to cook well. Whenever I stop at a restaurant while traveling, I go and look at the chef. If he's a thin fellow, I don't eat there."

Indeed, the *Houston Post* once called the cherubic Tony "our own Prince of Gastronomes." The original Prince of Gastronomes was Curnonsky, born Maurice-Edmond Sailland, a Frenchman through and through despite the pseudonym he adopted. The foremost epicure of his day, he was "a rotund, genial man with a gates-ajar collar, a twinkle in his eyes, and a prodigious gastronomic reputation," Samuel Chamberlain wrote in 1958. Tony to a T—if he would only wear gates-ajar collars.

When someone succeeds in reaching Tony on the telephone, the result may be wondrous. A woman called the restaurant one day, asked for Tony and was put through. A stranger, apparently not even a regular diner at the restaurant, she said she was giving a dinner party at her home and wondered if Tony would advise her. That he did, for fifteen minutes or more.

"I asked her what she wanted to serve for the main dish," Tony said long afterward. When she chose veal, Tony told her to go to

Jamail's, to ask for a certain butcher who was well-known to Tony and to say that he—Tony—had sent her. "Ask him to cut your veal chops the way mine are cut," he said, and then told her how to cook and serve the chops and what wine to serve (Puligny-Montrachet). A week or so later, she and her husband came to the restaurant for dinner. She thanked Tony again for his help, adding that the dinner had been a success.

In the popular mind, in the imagination of those who may never have been to Tony's, or who have been there only once or twice, the restaurant is thought of for spectacle, celebrities and Lucullan feasting. Few were surprised to read in the *Houston Chronicle* one Christmas season, in a list of luxury gifts called the Ultimate Gift Guide, that the second of nine suggestions was "An intimate dinner for four in Tony's wine cellar." The price of this *divertissement* was $3,500, or $875 a person. Still, the dinner was to include six rare wines, "enough Beluga caviar to belie its scarcity" and a many-course dinner, not to mention a string trio and, at the end, a 1947 Warre's Port.

Tony's has a knack for feeding the imagination other than in stimulating dreams of its food and wine glories. You hear that the restaurant's reservation lists and its accounting ledgers have been subpoenaed in big-rich divorce cases. You hear how one woman, in a magnificent fit of pique, had her trysting husband's Rolls-Royce towed from Tony's parking lot while her mate dined with another woman. Given time, the Tony's stories become legends, defying disbelief in their modern mythhood. But these fables have only a small role in the restaurant's distinction, which is revealed best in a slight alteration to those most sought-after words in the *Guide Michelin*: ". . . one of the best tables in America; *vaut le voyage*, worth a special journey."

'A Jug of Lafite . . .'

If you are ever at a loss to support
a flagging conversation, introduce the subject of eating.

LEIGH HUNT

THE COOKERY AT TONY'S is a blend of tradition and brilliant improvisation. It has been informed by, but has never cohered with, gastronomic fashion; nouvelle cuisine, the trendy California cuisine, the so-called *cuisine moderne* and the others each have had only as much influence on the restaurant's food style as Tony judges to be useful. Some of the restaurant's pasta and seafood combinations especially reveal its gustatory principles, and these dishes are at once elegant and humble.

"It is hard to make an exceptional dish with second-class ingredients," Tony says, "but it is easy to spoil the first-class ones. My restaurant is only as good as the last meal we have served." His restaurant is esteemed for many reasons, among which are its *pommes soufflées*. These light, magically puffed potatoes illustrate what may be called Tony Vallone's grit in mastering something that had baffled him. *Pommes soufflées* should never be served if they are greasy, which is usually the case. But properly done, they are a kind of merit badge for a restaurant.

"I used to fly to New Orleans in the middle sixties just to go to Antoine's to eat their *pommes soufflées*, trying to figure out how they did it," Tony says. "I badgered everybody there, but their success never came through to me." At length, a friend, a diner at Tony's from early days, gave him a leg up. Andre Crispin was a friend in need. "Andre helped me perfect the *pommes soufflées*," Tony says "as he helped me in many other ways." Tony does not recommend these for home cooking, however. "Like our pizza potatoes," he said, "making *pommes soufflées* is a little messy if you don't have really big fryers."

One reason this impeccable, opulent restaurant glows is the owner's nitpicking, fussbudgeting perfectionism, which also explains why Tony is such a tough customer. "If we don't get that big, super-lump Gulf crabmeat, I don't serve crabmeat," he says. "I serve only prime beef, but only if it has been aged twenty-one days. Most restaurants go eighteen; we require twenty-one to twenty-three, which is the Eastern standard. Our salmon is Gaspé and Scottish and Irish and Norwegian, not that mushy, oversalted belly lox that's such a horrible orange color."

Though once fairly shy and unsure of himself in his public role, Tony has come to relish his gastronome's mantle and its authority and responsibility. Vegetable bisque was being served to a friend one day. "Beauty and nutrition in one dish," he said. "Everything I can get fresh at market is minced—not fine, as you see, but fairly large—to make this dish. Then we finish it off with a little sherry, poured at table. I don't put onions in it," he said, adding a soupçon to the diner's pleasure in the dish.

Another time, another table, he was saying it takes eighteen hours to make *sauce espagnole,* which is the foundation of nearly all brown sauces and is known as the *sauce mère*, the mother sauce. "The most important thing on the plate is balance," he said. "Right now the new American chefs are in a phase that pays little heed to balance. The main dishes and the sauces in any given meal must balance and enhance each other, not compete with each other or mask the dish."

He is almost a sorcerer as diners gather. One day at lunch he went from table to table showing diners he knew, and a few strangers, the huge porcini (Italian mushrooms) he had just received. "Like huge cèpes," he said. "I grill them like a steak over live charcoal with a little lemon juice and a touch of butter." To an astringent woman who had never before been to Tony's but who had called him to her table to raise Cain before she had even seen the menu: "There is no way you can enjoy yourself here unless you have an open mind about us." To a table of four who had just been seated for lunch: "Try the Osso Buco—it's great." (Not one took his advice, ordering instead more costly dishes. So he sent a sample to the table.)

Any classification of restaurants is of course subjective and almost as personal as one's choice of a lover. *Di gustibus non est disputandum*—there is no disputing about tastes. One man goes to Tony's on a beautiful day with the woman he loves and they have a magnificent lunch. Later, he recommends Tony's to a friend, who takes a shrew to lunch on a stormy day after an important business matter has gone awry. The lunch is a catastrophe, and he never forgives his friend for sending him to Tony's. That's life—for a restaurateur. What had been sumptuous, lighthearted, all of a piece for one couple was a debacle for the other. By its inherent nature, dining asks not only the cook but also the diner to contribute to the art of dining.

"What a restaurant is, is details," Tony says. "The kitchen staff knows very well how to do the difficult things. It forgets the little things." Of the seventy men and women on the restaurant's staff, twenty-seven work in the kitchen: the executive chef, seven cooks, two butchers, three pantry women and the rest. You learn a lot about Tony's kitchen by knowing what is absent from it. None of the streamlined appurtenances starred in the wine, food and travel magazines are there: no microwave ovens, no heat lamps, no frozen food, no mixes. "Our freezer is full of bones," Tony says, bones used to make stocks and sauces. The restaurant does its own butchering, using twenty beef tenderloins and twenty-five to thirty racks of lamb every night, and around thirty-five legs of veal a week.

In the front, the service ratio is four men to seven tables—a captain, a front waiter, a kitchen waiter and a busman, plus three supervisors (the general manager, the manager and Tony himself) who all double as maître d's.

Travel/Holiday magazine has described the main dining room as "one of the most beautiful in America." The subdued splendor, the reserved sense of epicurean pleasure and black-tie European service inform every dinner. The overflowing abundance of fruits and vegetables, of meat and seafood, of wine and flowers on a great table at the entrance to the dining room illumine gastronomy—and invite it. The claret-colored walls and the starched white linen and the crystal are spiced by the vibrant colors of original French, German and American impressionist paintings. On the west wall is a priceless twenty-six-foot Chinese screen, circa 1690.

Above all, the dining room is flowery (does any other restaurant have a full-time florist on its staff?) in graceful counterpoint to the room's stateliness: a bouquet of fresh flowers on every table, banks of fresh flowers or plants dividing the room, and the huge bouquet atop the dessert cart. When dinner is done, the colors of the lovely pyramid of fresh fruits are brought to table—strawberries, two kinds of grapes, oranges, apples. This is the restaurant's thank-you to its diners. Everything—the food, the wine, the service, the atmosphere—may be described as of a sumptuous simplicity. For a little while, you can abolish time at Tony's.

It follows that Tony's has become a mecca for celebrities, some of whom seem to feel especially drawn to the restaurant—Helen Hayes, Jacqueline Bisset, Joan Rivers and John Travolta among them. The restaurant's awards include an unbroken string of *Travel/Holiday* awards ("This is one of the greatest restaurants in America . . . and is among the top-ranking of our Award candidates," the magazine said one year), a place on Dun's list of the top twenty restaurants in the United States and, for a time, it was the only Texas restaurant on *Playboy*'s choice of the twenty-five leading American restaurants. And Tony's has been cited by Julia Child, Simone Beck, Craig Claiborne, Paul Bocuse and Jean Troisgros.

A JUG OF LAFITE

Katherine S. Tapping, long a diner at Tony's, condensed all this into one line (recalling *The Rubaiyat of Omar Khayyam*) in a letter to a friend: "A jug of Lafite, a dinner at Tony's—and Thou."

Much has been written about the fetes and feasts that have taken place in Tony's wine cellar (one writer calling it "the womb-like, subterranean vault"), most of it exaggerated for readers' delight. What chiefly distinguishes the wine cellar is the art of dining, usually accompanied by many rather than one or two wines.

A JUG OF LAFITE

All eyes become thieves at dinners in the wine cellar: the ranks of crystal and the harvest of beauty of the big table's decorations of fresh fruits and vegetables and flowers. And the four walls lined with wine bins. Tony collects modern art, antique Chinese porcelains—and rare wine, much of which is in the cellar. But you become aware of the restaurant's remarkable wine cache before you reach the cellar or your table. As you enter Tony's you see on your right a small, refrigerated display case, where the rarest of wines are shown.

Every bottle is real and for sale, though with no expectation that any will ever be sold. The bottle of 1844 Château Lafite-Rothschild, priced at $17,500, is shown on the wine list, but the display case holds many wines not on the wine list, including a magnum of 1874 Château Mouton-Rothschild for $10,000, a magnum of 1945 Château Petrus for $4,000 and, the oldest wine in the case, an 1811 Vieux Cognac for $10,000.

The text at the head of the "Indulgence" section of Tony's wine list reads: "These collector's wines . . . are epicure's wines, the cream. They are among the most distinguished and rarest in America, and they have been treated with the respect they deserve. Because of their age, however, they must be served at the purchaser's risk."

Ah! Suppose someone buys the 1962 Cheval Blanc for $275 and it turns out to be vinegar—farfetched indeed for a fairly young classic Bordeaux red. Would he or she have to pay $275 for less than a quart of vinegar? No one knows, for that has never occurred, but it seems most unlikely. Does anyone ever buy these wines? Occasionally someone buys a bottle from the top of the Indulgence list, where wines are priced under $500. One exception was a bottle of 1919 Chateau Haut-Brion for $1,500; a son bought it for his father's birthday because 1919 was the year of the father's birth.

Nearly all of these collector's wines are represented by more than a single bottle, and some by more than half a case. Why would

Tony go to such extravagant lengths to join so many glorious bottles? "I wanted to assemble an authentic collection of the greatest bottles extant." And yet, prices on his wine list begin at $16, with many bottles priced from $20 to $35.

A JUG OF LAFITE

Like every great restaurant, Tony's and wine are indivisible, but Tony Vallone's sense of wine is perhaps simpler—perhaps more Italian—than that of most leading restaurateurs. He was asked to write an article about wine in 1978. "I would say," he wrote, "that the pleasures of wine require but two conditions: an open mind and some knowledge of the distinction between eating and dining." And then, addressing a favorite subject: "The so-called wine mystique is humbug. When you are drinking or talking about wine, what matters are common sense and curiosity. We should take wine as a matter of course, as being a co-equal part of a meal with bread and meat, not as something to be revered more or less than we revere bread and meat."

Advice to the Stovelorn

That all-softening, overpowering knell,
The tocsin of the soul—the dinner bell.
LORD BYRON

Ponder well on this point: the pleasant hours of our life
are all connected by a more or less tangible link
with some memory of the table.
CHARLES MONSELET

WISELY JUDGING THAT FRIENDS and diners who ask for cooking tips are really hoping to learn how to turn a bowl of rice into fresh Beluga caviar, Tony tries to avoid their questions. "Nor do I ever suggest shortcuts, because I know of none that does justice to a dish, let alone improves it," he says. "Shortcuts and good cookery are mutually exclusive. They cancel each other out." The qualifying word is "good." "There are thousands of shortcuts in cooking, but none in good cookery because, for one thing among many, there is no shortcut to patience," he says. "Patience is an essential ingredient of good cookery that is always absent from the recipe."

But of course a professional in anything can tick off little things learned from the experience of a flood of years. Of these, Tony calls one cooking tip fundamental: "If you don't have it, don't make it.

First, go to the store and get it." Which is to say, *no substitutions*. "Milk does not cook like cream," he says. "This is where many cooks blunder. Unless you know from experience that you have a better way, follow the recipe. Not that the recipes are sacred, not that they cannot be altered and improved," he says. "You must always leave room for inspiration, for intuition." When it comes to cooking, he says, "I have always been from the trial-and-error school."

ADVICE TO THE STOVELORN

After cooking many of the dishes in the recipe chapters, Jean Hardy offers a droll—and sound—cautionary note: "Certain things you must stock up on when you use this book." These certain things are:

- A fruity Italian extra virgin olive oil.
- Good imported Italian canned tomatoes.
- High-quality imported pasta.
- Much more fresh garlic than you are accustomed to buying.
- Balsamic vinegar.
- Red wine vinegar.
- Two pepper mills, one for white pepper, one for black.
- Seasoned salt (Tony likes Lawry's).
- A bottle of dry white vermouth and another of white wine.
- Unsalted butter.

In addition, you will need to locate dependable sources of fresh basil, and sweet red and yellow peppers. You will, moreover, need to change your grocery shopping patterns. You will find yourself looking for the purveyors of the freshest seafood, the crispiest arugula and the cleverest cuts of lamb and veal. In a word, the serious student of this book will be embarking on an adventure. And if the list sounds a mite Italian, "blame it on my Sorrentino culinary upbringing," says Tony.

Some diners feel that the restaurant's striking dessert soufflés, which reach amazing heights, are made with some kind of charm or spell. One woman, herself a gifted cook, has three words for them: "Soufflés without fear," adding, "What is the secret of these marvelous soufflés? Soufflés are not all that mysterious, and yet—how does Tony do it?"

This is what he says about making a high-rising soufflé that stays risen until served: First, whip the egg whites fairly stiff with a pinch of cream of tartar. Second, *never* mix well the egg whites into the soufflé mixture; just barely fold the two together. "It will be uneven in cooking," he says, "but it will cook out perfectly."

ADVICE TO THE STOVELORN

Cooking with wine, Tony feels, is widely misunderstood. First of all, there is no such thing as a "cooking" wine. "If the wine isn't good enough for you to drink with pleasure, it isn't good enough to cook with, either," he says. To use a spoiled or a cheap wine in cookery is costly rather than thrifty, for such wine only brings out the wine's faults in the finished and thus usually spoiled dish.

Not that Tony suggests using an expensive wine in cooking, nor does he do so at the restaurant. Noting that wine's alcohol cooks away, he suggests finding a moderately priced regional wine of France, Italy, or the United States or whatever you like to drink. "If you enjoy drinking the wine," he says, "the chances are it will be a good cooking wine." What cookery wants is a full-bodied, flavorful wine.

Tony and seafood are as hand in glove. Though he is esteemed for his veal dishes, his lamb and pasta, for his desserts and his wines, it seems likely that his most influential culinary work has been in creating seafood masterpieces. Call this an Italian instinct, an Italian gift, for no place in Italy is very far from the sea. Moreover, though he skillfully prepares the rich seafood dishes that some dinners require, he reaches his apogee in his rapport with simple, grilled, lightly sauced swordfish, red snapper, redfish and Gulf sea trout. And count on him above all in his uses of the region's blue crab, the diamond of Texas cuisine.

So, Tony speaks ex cathedra on seafood:

"There is an Italian saying, '*L'ospite e' come il pesce dopo; tre giorni, puzza,*'" he says. "Guests are like fish; in three days they stink." In buying any dead fish, saltwater or fresh, he says, look for a bright and staring eye. The fish must not feel slimy; its flesh, poked with a finger, should spring back as does a healthy human's flesh. Above all, a fish should *smell* fresh, not fishy. When fillets are wanted, it is always best to choose the whole fish and have it filleted on the spot. That way you can be sure it is fresh as possible.

Shrimp, like fresh finfish, should have no objectionable odor and no sign of deterioration—no black spots, no freezer burn. For an appetizer at lunch one day, Tony ordered a grilled shrimp dish for his guests. When it was served, he sent it right back to the kitchen. "There was too much butter—about half would be right—but, more than that, you must char the shell a little. That's where the flavor comes from."

On sole: "The funny thing about sole," he says, "is that it may be the only fish that's not at its best the instant it's caught. Cook it right off and the flesh will be hard, not appetizing. You have to keep it two or three days before it is at its best—though of course this isn't much of a problem in the Gulf Coast region."

On anchovy: "The fresh fish, which we rarely see, is excellent, but it is nothing like the flavor of the cured anchovy. The special value of cured anchovy is that it sharpens the appetite for meat and drink. When used with other fish and some fowl, it heightens their flavors, too. Anchovies are also fabulous with sliced tomatoes—just add olive oil, lemon juice and a pinch of oregano and basil."

Tony's choices of seasonings and condiments are those of a professional who has experimented for years. "As a rule," he says, "when a recipe calls for salt, I use Lawry's Seasoned Salt rather than plain salt."

"Balsamic vinegar, now. I especially like Williams-Sonoma's Fini as a superior balsamic vinegar. For the money, it's the best." (Balsamic vinegar is a dark, richly flavored vinegar that comes from Italy's Modena region.)

Choosing the correct olive oil is essential to Tony's cookery; extra virgin olive oils with fruity flavor are preferred. Tony makes four recommendations, the first costly, the others less so: either Ranieri or Antinori (one of Italy's premier winemakers as well) first, and then Colavita or Madre Sicilia or—Tony's favorite—Amastra, an oil he imports from Italy for restaurant use. Use a better oil as an ingredient in a dish and a less expensive oil for frying or sautéing, Tony advises. Olive oil, being monounsaturated, can have a glorious effect on your palate, but none at all on your arteries. Which is one more reason for its exalted place in cuisine. "You may substitute vegetable oils if you wish," Tony says, "but your food will not taste the same."

On wine vinegar: "I always use red wine vinegar," Tony says. "Though I prefer many of the less common imported Italian brands, Regina and Progresso are also excellent."

ADVICE TO THE STOVELORN

"In cooking," Tony says, "go in whatever direction your taste leans, whether that means more of something, or less. In culinary terms, a pinch is defined as the amount of something that can be held between the thumb and forefinger, but I say it is whatever it takes to get the flavor you want. Please *your* palate first."

Of course, and yet . . .

Tony has more kitchen experience than most, so let's go to class. Tony is the lecturer:

"The whole secret of cooking spinach is not to cook it too long—a minute or less, never more."

"That leaf of basil [on a dish a diner had been served]—eat it. Always eat the basil on your plate. It keeps the breath good, especially if you've been eating garlic. And it tastes good."

"I think most cream soups should have a little sherry added just before serving."

"Pan-frying a steak has many advantages, and it is the most practical way to cook any steak that is less than an inch thick."

"Baking a potato wrapped in aluminum foil makes a steamed rather than a baked potato because the foil traps the moisture escaping from the skin. Don't bake your potatoes in foil."

"In sautéing garlic, don't let it brown; cook it until it is opaque. Handled correctly, garlic is sweet and aromatic, not pungent and bitter."

"Nothing piquants a sauce like crushed red peppers—but be careful because they're hot."

"The only herb I prefer dry instead of fresh is oregano. It just seems to work better used in very small amounts and at the end of cooking a dish."

"I much prefer the ripe red and yellow peppers to green pep-

pers. I use green peppers only in gumbo and a few other Cajun dishes."

"Italian flat-leaved parsley has more flavor than the curly kind. Use it whenever you have it available."

"As a rule, homemade bread is no longer as good as good bakery bread. A good crusty French or Italian loaf is never a mistake. When I can't get Italian loaves that suit me, I buy the round French country loaves, called *pain de campagne*, which most nearly resemble Italian-style bread."

"Marinating meat and vegetables in wine or in a mixture of wine and spices is often worth doing for more dishes than the few recipes that specify it. Wine transforms food. It makes meat more tender, wonderfully flavors it and gives a delicious sauce. I say meat and vegetables because I don't much believe in marinating fish."

"Cilantro is important in Mexican and Middle Eastern cooking, but it has no place in the Italian kitchen, and certainly no place in any delicate sauce or dish." (Howard Hillman's *The Cook's Book* says, under Coriander, "The green, lacy leaves—also known as *Chinese parsley* or *cilantro*—have a pungent and distinctive odor that some American and European palates consider an acquired taste.")

"When I call for fresh tomatoes, I mean overripe tomatoes. The redder they are, the better they cook. And I prefer the San Marzano variety or other imported Italian [canned] tomatoes, which are richer and tastier than our own. The best is the Luigi Vitelli brand, but it is hard to find. The Zia Dora or Progresso brands are the best Italian tomatoes available in our markets."

"The imported Italian pastas are far superior to American pastas. They are faster cooking and lighter and, most important, 'toothier.' My favorite brands are De Cecco and Gerardo di Nola."

"One hard-to-find but excellent pasta to use, and both De Cecco and Gerardo di Nola make it, is fidelini, which is slightly larger than angel hair—*capellini d'angeli*—but finer than most other pastas. Fidelini is the perfect pasta. It and linguine are my favorites. Finally, I prefer dried pastas with the heavier tomato sauces and fresh pastas with milder cream sauces."

PART TWO

The Recipes

Appetizers

My idea of heaven is eating *pâté de foie gras*
to the sound of trumpets.
SYDNEY SMITH

AN OLD SOUTHERN SAYING that "Eating is the pleasure of the poor" tells us only part of the story, for eating is the pleasure of all who are healthy. And it occupies us far more than we may think. Arnold Bennett wrote that a person of sixty has spent more than three years of his or her life in eating. "Between the ages of twenty and fifty," M.F.K. Fisher wrote, "John Doe spends some twenty thousand hours chewing and swallowing food, more than eight hundred days and nights of steady eating."

Neither of these intimidating speculations takes account of the additional time—months, really, overall—needed to plan, acquire and cook what is to be eaten, let alone to clean up afterward. Small wonder that many of us do indeed live to eat! Well, here is a bookful of ways to spend some of that time, beginning in this chapter with appetizers.

Do many still think of an appetizer in the original sense of "something to soothe and at the same time to excite the palate"? That seems unlikely. Appetizers have become small (and not always small) versions of main courses. Many of us have had whole dinners consisting only of two or three, maybe four, appetizers, which is called "grazing."

. . . pâté de foie gras to the sound of trumpets.

Indeed, Tony reminds that many of the ensuing appetizers may also be served as main courses by enlarging the portions. But this metamorphosis of the appetizer ("a bit of something that excites a desire for more," one dictionary says) into substance in its own right is dining's loss. Still, insofar as fashion gives him elbow room, Tony has adhered to the appetizer's classic concept of "something to excite the palate," as being a bridge to the dishes to come.

One of the most delicately lovely of Tony's caviar appetizers is almost too simple to need a recipe—Beggars' Purses, perhaps the only time beggars become choosers. Beggars' Purses are served only at some wine cellar dinners because preparation must begin well in advance of serving. Nothing to them, really, except poetry: tiny, paper-thin crêpes filled with fresh Beluga caviar and *crème fraîche* and tied up with the bright green of tiny leek strips.

Tony's Pâté

This justly celebrated pâté has been served for many years to all Tony's diners soon after they are seated. It is surprisingly easy to make at home and keeps well in the refrigerator.

4 pounds chicken livers
1 pound softened butter
1½ pounds chopped onion
1 tablespoon salt
3 cloves garlic, minced
2 teaspoons crushed dried or fresh rosemary
2 teaspoons dried thyme
1½ teaspoons dried marjoram
1 teaspoon freshly ground pepper
2 cups Armagnac

In a large skillet, melt half the butter, then add onions and sauté 10 minutes, or until onions are translucent. Stir in livers and sauté until they are light brown on the outside and pink on the inside. Add salt, garlic, rosemary, thyme, marjoram and pepper and continue to cook 3–5 minutes. Stir in Armagnac and remove from heat. Let cool, stirring often. Blend in food processor until very smooth. Place in a large bowl over ice and whip constantly, until mixture thickens slightly and becomes cloudy.

Add remaining softened butter a little at a time, whipping constantly. Mixture will become thick and creamy. Fill a pâté crock or suitable bowl. Cover well and refrigerate at least 1, preferably 2 days, before serving. Serve with toasted bread rounds or crusty fresh bread. Ideal for a large party.

WINE: *Cahors (a French red), a sparkling wine or a Sauternes*

Quick Chicken Liver Pâté with Juniper Berries

1 pound chicken livers
2 tablespoons butter
3 tablespoons Italian extra virgin olive oil
2 or 3 slices prosciutto, chopped
2 teaspoons minced sage leaves or *½ teaspoon dried sage*
1 bay leaf
5 or 6 juniper berries, ground to a powder
2 cloves garlic, crushed in a garlic press
Seasoned salt and freshly ground black pepper
1 tablespoon capers

Clean and chop the chicken livers. Melt the butter with the olive oil in a skillet over low heat. Add the chicken livers, prosciutto, sage, bay leaf, juniper berries, garlic, salt and pepper. Cook for about 10 minutes or just until cooked through. Let cool.

Purée mixture in a food processor by pulsing quickly. (For a smoother, lighter texture, purée a tablespoon of softened butter with the mixture. A teaspoon of brandy added at the same time can add some extra zip to this dish, which has endless variations.)

Turn into a small bowl or serving dish. Garnish with capers and chill well.

WINE: *Beaujolais or Barbera d'Asti (the Italian Beaujolais) or a Sauternes*

Tony's Fish Mousse with Rose Petals

Preparation of this dish takes too long for it to be on the menu, Tony says, "but it is a great dish for parties in the wine cellar—and you may eat the rose petals. If you want to make a memorable impression, this is the dish to go with."

1 pound of fresh trout or redfish, filleted (save bones and trimmings for stock)
1 cup very thick béchamel (3 tablespoons butter, 3 tablespoons flour and 1 cup cream or half-and-half)
Seasoned salt and generous pinch white pepper
1 teaspoon nutmeg
1 teaspoon lemon juice
1 tablespoon grated orange zest
1 whole egg plus 2 yolks
½ cup whipping cream
Rose petals

Purée trout in a food processor using the metal blade. Mix fish and béchamel and rub together through a sieve. Add salt, pepper, nutmeg, lemon juice, orange zest (just the orange part of the rind, no white), egg, egg yolks and cream, and mix well. Turn into well-buttered ½-cup molds, and place in pan of hot water. Bake in a preheated 325° oven until knife inserted comes out clean (about 30 minutes). Remove mold from oven and water bath. Turn out on a serving plate. Cool. Insert rose petals in layers around edges of mold to re-create rose shape, and top with leaf or heart of rose. Serves 8 as first course.

WINE: *A late-harvest Riesling*

Crabmeat Remick

Tony's version of a classic New Orleans dish.

2 pounds fresh lump crabmeat
1–1½ cups mayonnaise
5 tablespoons chili sauce
6–8 drops Tabasco sauce
1 tablespoon prepared mustard
½ teaspoon seasoned salt
½ teaspoon black pepper
1 tablespoon lemon juice
1 tablespoon butter
½ cup bread crumbs

Place crabmeat on bottom of a buttered casserole (or in individual ramekins). Combine mayonnaise and seasonings. Spread mixture over the crabmeat and sprinkle with the bread crumbs. Place dish in a preheated oven under the broiler close to the heat (about 3 inches) and broil for about 5 minutes or until browned and the crabmeat is warmed through. (Do not let the crabmeat dry out.)

This is a good chafing dish item for a buffet menu. Crackers or toast can accompany. Serves 10–12.

WINE: *Pinot Grigio or a white Zinfandel, both spicy, or a fruity Muscadet*

Crabmeat with Dill

5 cups lump crabmeat
1 cup shallots, minced
3 tablespoons butter
2 cloves garlic, minced
1 cup dry sherry
5 egg yolks, mixed well
2½ cups warm béchamel (recipe on page 150)
2 tablespoons fresh dill, chopped fine
2 tablespoons chopped fresh parsley
Cayenne to taste
Seasoned salt and freshly ground white pepper

In a heavy saucepan sauté the shallots in the butter, stirring for about 2 minutes. Add the garlic and sauté, stirring until the shallots are limp and the garlic opaque. Add the sherry and bring to a boil. Let mixture reduce a little, then add the crabmeat. Toss gently but well. Blend the egg yolks into the béchamel and add this to the crabmeat, stirring gently. Add dill, parsley, cayenne, salt, and white pepper. Serve immediately in a chafing dish or spooned onto individual plates. Toast or crackers make a good accompaniment. Serves 6–8.

Note: This dish has many variations. Sweet basil can be substituted for dill, mushrooms or broccoli florets can be added, mustard can be added to the sauce, and on and on. Be creative—have fun with this one.

WINE: *Müller-Thurgau, Pouilly-Fumé or Mâcon (white)*

Soft-shell Crabs with Lime Sauce

8 medium-sized soft-shell crabs
½ cup flour seasoned with 1 teaspoon seasoned salt and 1 teaspoon black pepper
½ pound butter
Grated rind and juice of 2 limes
½ cup white wine or dry vermouth
Additional seasoned salt, black pepper
Lime slices

Coat the crabs with the seasoned flour and shake off any excess. Sauté the crabs in half the hot butter for about 2 minutes on each side. Remove crabs and keep warm. Discard grease from pan.

Add the wine to the pan, and 1 minute later add the lime rind and juice. Deglaze the pan by scraping all the browned particles with a wooden spoon and incorporating them into the liquid. Keep mixing and allow sauce to reduce a little. Add remaining butter. Season to taste with seasoned salt and pepper. Pour some sauce over each crab, garnish with lime and serve immediately. Serves 4–8.

WINE: *Verdicchio or Gavi*

Shrimp Tony's

One to one and one-half pounds crabmeat may be substituted for the shrimp.

6 tablespoons butter
3 or 4 cloves garlic, minced
18 large shrimp, butterflied, with tails left on
2 cups sliced fresh mushrooms
1½ cups whipping cream
1 tablespoon tomato paste
6 tablespoons sweet sherry
1 tablespoon tarragon
Cayenne pepper
Loose handful of fresh basil
3 tablespoons brandy
Seasoned rice ring

Melt butter in a saucepan over medium heat. Add garlic and sauté briefly, about 2–3 minutes. Do not let garlic brown! Add shrimp and sauté just until they begin to color. Remove shrimp. Add mushrooms and sauté very briefly, only until they are about half cooked. Remove the mushrooms. Next add cream, tomato paste, sherry and tarragon, and let simmer until sauce is reduced and slightly thickened.

Return shrimp and mushrooms to pan. Add a pinch or two of cayenne pepper and heat through. If fresh basil is available (and it is preferred), shred or tear it into pieces and add it now. (If you use dried basil, add it when you add the tarragon.) Warm brandy over the stove in a small saucepan and pour over sauce and ignite, stirring until flames subside.

Spoon shrimp and sauce into the center of a seasoned rice ring and serve immediately. Serves 6.

WINE: *A white Rhône, either Côtes-du-Rhône or Crozes-Hermitage*

Shrimp with Ricotta

½ cup minced onion
1½ tablespoons butter
1½ tablespoons olive oil
½ cup dry Marsala or dry red wine
4–5 ripe medium tomatoes, peeled, seeded and chopped
2 cloves garlic, minced
1 teaspoon seasoned salt
⅓ teaspoon freshly ground pepper
¾ teaspoon oregano
4 ounces ricotta, at room temperature
1 pound very large shrimp, shelled and deveined
¼ cup chopped fresh parsley

In a heavy skillet, sauté onion in butter and oil until soft. Add wine, tomatoes, garlic, salt, pepper and oregano. Bring to a boil, lower heat and simmer, stirring occasionally until sauce is slightly thickened. Stir in cheese and simmer for 10 minutes. Adjust seasoning.

Just before serving, add the shrimp to the hot sauce and cook for 5 minutes or until the shrimp are just tender. Do not overcook. Garnish with parsley and serve immediately with crusty French or Italian bread. Serves 4.

WINE: *Grignolino, Meursault or Sancerre*

Shrimp in Mustard Sauce

24 large fresh shrimp
2–3 tablespoons oil
2 shallots, minced
½ cup dry white vermouth or wine
½ cup whipping cream
1 cup unsalted butter, cut into chunks
2 tablespoons coarse French mustard or creole mustard
Salt and freshly ground pepper
Fresh lemon juice

Shell and devein raw shrimp. Heat oil in large heavy skillet until very hot. Add shrimp in batches and stir-fry 1–2 minutes. (Shrimp should be underdone.) Using slotted spoon, remove shrimp from skillet and set aside.

Reduce heat to medium, add more oil to skillet if necessary and sauté shallots 30 seconds. Pour in wine, scraping up any browned bits. Stir in cream. Cook, stirring until mixture thickens slightly (about 4–5 minutes). Reduce heat to low and gradually whisk in butter, then whisk in mustard (do not let boil). Add salt, pepper and a squeeze of fresh lemon juice. Pour over shrimp and serve immediately. Serves 8.

WINE: *Chablis or Pineau des Charentes*

Shrimp Vermouth

2 pounds fresh shrimp
1½ cups dry white vermouth
½ cup white vinegar
⅓ cup thinly sliced onion
⅓ cup thinly sliced celery
⅓ cup thinly sliced carrots
3 sprigs parsley
1 bay leaf
¼ teaspoon dried thyme
5 cloves garlic, sliced
¼ teaspoon dried oregano
Generous pinch crushed red pepper flakes
Pinch seasoned salt
6–8 whole black peppercorns

Peel the shrimp and butterfly them, leaving the tails on. Simmer the remaining ingredients in a large saucepan for 15 minutes. Add the shrimp, cover the pan and let cook/steam for 4 minutes, shaking the pan frequently. Serve immediately or let shrimp cool in cooking liquid and use later. Do not overcook the shrimp. Serve on individual plates and spoon a little of the pan juices and vegetables over the shrimp. Serves 6–8.

WINE: *A late-harvest Rhine or Chablis*

Orange, Italian Homestyle, and Pepper salads

Baked Scallops Radicchio

18 large scallops (with roe, if available)
Seasoned salt
Freshly ground white pepper
Juice of 2 lemons
16 radicchio leaves
1½ tablespoons unsalted butter
2 shallots, chopped fine
1 medium garlic clove, chopped fine
2 cups dry white vermouth or wine

Place scallops in a bowl. Sprinkle with seasoned salt and pepper and pour the lemon juice over. Let marinate 15 minutes, turning occasionally. Preheat oven to 450°.

Blanch radicchio leaves in boiling water just until wilted, about 1 minute or less. Immediately immerse in cold water to stop cooking process. Dry each leaf thoroughly and wrap one leaf around each scallop.

In an ovenproof skillet large enough to hold the scallops, melt butter. Over medium heat sauté shallots and garlic until shallots are translucent (about 3 minutes). Add the wine and reduce by half.

Arrange the scallops in the skillet and transfer to the oven. Bake 3–4 minutes, basting once or twice with the pan juice. Serve immediately, garnished with lemon wedges. Serves 6.

WINE: *Pinot Grigio*

Herb-fried Squid or Octopus

Waverley Root notes in his *The Best of Italian Cooking* that squid and octopus are "much eaten in Italy but little liked, to put it mildly, in, for instance, America and England. . . ." One reason for this, he says, is that these seafoods are rare in U.S. and British waters. However, Tony believes fresh squid and even octopus are now coming into their own in the U.S. "I was raised on squid and can't imagine doing without it," he says.

2 cups uncooked squid rings or *tentacle meat from a cooked 3–3½ pound octopus, cut into bite-size pieces* or *a combination of both squid and octopus*
2 eggs, well-beaten
Freshly ground black pepper
1½ cups Italian-style dried bread crumbs
¼ teaspoon dried oregano
½ teaspoon dried basil
½ teaspoon dried thyme
1½ tablespoons grated Parmesan cheese
Olive oil to fill a skillet to depth of 1 inch
Lemon wedges (or pesto)

Season the beaten eggs well with fresh pepper. In another bowl, mix well the bread crumbs, herbs and cheese.

Dip each piece of squid or octopus in the egg mixture. Fry the seafood in well-heated oil until golden brown on both sides, about 5 minutes for octopus and less for squid.

Drain the fried seafood on paper towels and serve with lemon wedges or with pesto (see recipe on page 76). Serves 4.

WINE: *Corvo (a bone-dry, austere Sicilian white) or Pinot Grigio*

Gravlax all' Italiana

1 whole fresh salmon, about 3–3½ pounds
2 tablespoons fennel seeds
2 tablespoons sugar
Seasoned salt and freshly ground black pepper
2 tablespoons fresh chopped dill
4 ounces cognac or Grappa (or a little more if desired)
5–6 mint sprigs, leaves only

Ask your butcher to fillet the salmon, leaving the skin on; you want 2 nice, large fillets. Make sure he removes the bones from the fish.

Mix the fennel seeds and sugar in a small bowl. Place one fillet, skin side down, in a glass or enamel baking dish. Generously salt and pepper the fillet. Next, rub the fennel/sugar mixture well into the fish flesh. Next, sprinkle the dill over the fish, then sprinkle the cognac, and place the mint leaves over all. Season the second salmon fillet with salt and pepper and sprinkle a little cognac on the flesh. Place the second fillet, skin side up, on top of the first.

Cover the fish with wax paper and then cover tightly with plastic wrap. Set a plate and then a heavy object (2–3 pounds) on top of the fish to weight it down. Let the fish "cure" in the refrigerator (turning it daily) for 5 days. Before serving, lift the fish from the juices that will have collected. Remove the herbs from between the fillets and wipe the fillets dry. To serve, carve the fillets on a diagonal into paper-thin slices, with pumpernickel slices alongside. A good party dish.

WINE: *Oregon white Riesling or Frascati (Crispin: "Oregon winegrower David Lett says the perfect marriage is his Eyrie Vineyard's white Riesling and salmon.")*

Marinated Eggplant

Tony: "Refreshing—and the longer you keep it, the better it gets."

5 or 6 Italian or Japanese eggplants
Fruity Italian olive oil for frying
1 large bunch fresh basil leaves
5 cloves garlic, chopped fine
½ cup red wine vinegar

Cut off the stem and blossom ends of the eggplants. Cut lengthwise thin slices about ¼ inch thick (there is no need to salt and drain these small eggplants).

Pour enough olive oil to cover the bottom of a skillet. Fry the eggplants, removing slices from the pan as soon as they brown. Do not let them get mushy.

Note: You might prefer to grill these eggplants; the grilled flavor and markings add a lot to the dish and less oil is used. Dip the slices in olive oil and place on the hot charcoal grill. Turn to mark them with a crisscross pattern, and grill a minute or so in each position on both sides.

In a glass or enamel baking dish, make a layer of eggplant slices. Sprinkle some of the basil and garlic and a good dash of the vinegar over them. Make another layer of the eggplant and repeat the sprinkling of herbs and vinegar. Continue until all the eggplant is layered and topped with herbs and vinegar. Cover with plastic wrap and refrigerate overnight or for at least 8 hours. Serves 4–6.

Stuffed Eggplant

8 baby Italian eggplants
½ cup Italian olive oil
½ cup chicken broth

Seasoned salt
½ loaf Italian or French bread, coarsely torn
1 pint heavy cream
12 ounces sweet Italian sausage meat (removed from casing)
1 teaspoon chopped garlic
1 egg yolk
1 cup freshly grated Romano cheese
1 tablespoon chopped fresh parsley
1 teaspoon thyme
Pinch oregano
Freshly ground black pepper
Pinch crushed red pepper
½ cup Italian-style bread crumbs

Cut off stems and blossom ends of eggplants and cut in half lengthwise. Leaving shells about ¼ inch thick, scoop out the pulp and set aside. Place eggplants skin down in a baking pan. Pour ¼ cup olive oil and ¼ cup broth over them, sprinkle with salt and set aside.

Soak bread in the cream for 30 minutes. Sauté the sausage over low heat in its own fat, stirring and breaking with a fork. When the sausage meat is brown, add the garlic and sauté for a minute or so more. Set aside.

Finely chop half of the eggplant pulp and discard the rest. Shred and knead the softened bread until it is almost a paste. In a mixing bowl, combine bread, egg yolk, cheese, sausage, parsley, thyme, oregano, both peppers, and eggplant pulp. Mix well.

Place eggplant shells in a preheated 350° oven and bake 15 minutes. Drain off liquid completely. Cool shells, stuff with mixture. Sprinkle with dried bread crumbs. Pour remaining oil and broth into pan. Place stuffed eggplant in pan and bake 20 minutes more (discard juice). Serves 8.

WINE: *Gavi or Frascati*

Eggplant Rollatini

A very popular appetizer at Tony's and a must for cheese lovers.

1 large purple eggplant
Salt and pepper
Italian olive oil for frying
Flour for dredging
3 tablespoons unsalted butter
2 small leeks, white parts only, chopped
2 ounces prosciutto, minced
2 ounces sun-dried tomatoes (in oil), chopped
¾ pound ricotta
¼ pound grated mozzarella cheese
1 ounce freshly grated Parmesan cheese
1 egg
Pinch of freshly grated nutmeg
2 cups béchamel (recipe on page 150)
2 cups marinara sauce (recipe on page 86)

Cut eggplant diagonally into ¼-inch-thick slices that are as long as possible. Lightly sprinkle eggplant slices on both sides with salt. Let stand in colander for 20 minutes. Rinse quickly under cold water and drain well.

Heat ¼ inch of olive oil in a large frying pan. Sprinkle eggplant with pepper and dredge in flour, shaking off excess. Fry slices in the hot olive oil (do not overcrowd) until golden brown, 1–2 minutes per side. Replenish olive oil as necessary. Drain the eggplant well on paper towels.

Melt butter in a small frying pan. Sauté leeks over medium heat for 1 minute, add prosciutto and sun-dried tomatoes and continue sautéing until leeks are soft, about 2 or 3 minutes.

Put cheeses in a bowl and beat in the leek mixture and egg. Season to taste with nutmeg, salt and pepper.

Preheat oven to 350° and butter a large baking dish. Spread a few tablespoons of the cheese mixture on each eggplant slice and roll the slice into a cylinder. Spread enough of a favorite cream sauce (preferably béchamel) on the bottom of the baking dish. Place the eggplant cylinders in the dish, then top them with more of the cream sauce and top that with the marinara sauce. Let some of the marinara spill to the bottom of the dish. Bake about 30–35 minutes. Serves 4–6.

WINE: *Pinot Grigio or Chianti*

Spinach Balls

2 cups cooked, chopped spinach
½ cup grated Parmesan cheese
½ pound ricotta
1 clove garlic, crushed in a garlic press
1 egg
Pinch nutmeg
Seasoned salt and freshly ground white pepper
Flour
6–8 chicken bouillon cubes
Sauce

Drain spinach well. Combine spinach, Parmesan, ricotta, garlic, egg and seasonings (using an extra pinch of white pepper). Mix thoroughly. Let sit at least 1 hour. Using a tablespoon, form spinach into balls and then roll them in flour, shaking off any excess.

Bring 3 quarts water to a boil with the bouillon cubes thrown in. Put 4 or 5 of the spinach balls into the boiling chicken stock, lower heat and simmer about 5 minutes. Remove with a slotted spoon and add the next batch of the spinach balls.

Serve in a chafing dish with tomato or cream sauce or a combination of both. Serves 10–12.

Stuffed Mushrooms Trastevere

This recipe comes from a restaurant in the Trastevere section of Rome. The mushrooms are particularly good served with marinara sauce.

8–12 large mushrooms
1 teaspoon salt
1 lemon, halved
6 paper-thin slices prosciutto
6 thin slices Genoa salami
2–3 large cloves garlic, minced
2 tablespoons chopped parsley
Good pinch of thyme
Good pinch of oregano
Good pinch of sage
3 sweet basil leaves, coarsely chopped
1 teaspoon freshly ground black pepper
1–2 tablespoons Italian-style bread crumbs
1½ cups grated Parmesan cheese
1 cup chicken broth

Carefully break off the mushroom stems without damaging the mushroom caps. Bring a pot of water to a boil, add the salt, squeeze both lemon halves in the water, then drop the lemons in the water. Add the mushroom caps and cook for 3 minutes. Drain.

Chop mushroom stems, prosciutto and salami as fine as possible and mix well with the garlic, parsley, herbs and pepper. Next, mix in 1 tablespoon bread crumbs, 1 cup of cheese and a sprinkling of the chicken broth. Use only as much stock as is necessary to moisten the mixture. Stuff mushrooms and arrange in a pan, stuffed side up. Pour remaining broth on bottom of pan. Bake in a preheated 350° oven for 10–15 minutes. Sprinkle remaining Parmesan cheese over mushrooms and broil for 3 minutes. Serve immediately. Serves 4–6.

WINE: *Zinfandel (red) or Chianti*

Salads

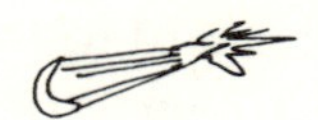

According to the Spanish proverb, four persons
are wanted to make a good salad: a spendthrift for oil,
a miser for vinegar, a counselor for salt and
a madman to stir it all up.

ABRAHAM HAYWARD

THE RANGE OF DISHES that have come to be called salads has increased so much that almost any dish except a soup or a dessert is now called salad by someone. Come to that, gazpacho, which traditionally combines cucumber, tomatoes, onions and sweet pepper, is also known as Spanish salad soup. Nothing is sacred to salads. From the simple green salad of lettuce or watercress to fearsome flights of fancy that often seem meant to usurp the place of the main course, salads have become a cuisine unto themselves.

The basic salad the world over is—or should be—some combination of olive oil, vinegar, salt, pepper and lettuce. This simple salad is charged with ritual, as it deserves to be: pull the lettuce leaves apart with your hands, wash them under cold water, break them into smaller pieces with your fingers. *Never use a knife.* And so on. But the purity of this salad is becoming lost in a kaleidoscope of invention, some of it admirable, more of it fit for oblivion.

Whether the salad is served as a first course or after the main course is in some circles a philosophical dispute that takes prece-

SALADS

dence over such lesser concerns as religion, politics and the libido. The American preference for salad as a first course, now sometimes accepted in Europe, has much to recommend it if wine is to be served with the main course. Speaking of northern California, M.F.K. Fisher has written that "there they are much influenced by fellow countrymen of French and Italian descent who would never cut into a good wine's attack on human taste buds by adding vinegar or lemon juice or even mustard to the battle." That amounts to acceptance of salad as a first course by the author of *The Art of Eating*.

Note: If you want to drink wine with a salad, choose a light, dry, white wine. Tony prefers a good mineral water such as Fiuggi.

. . . and a madman to stir it all up.

Caponata Siciliana

This Sicilian-style eggplant salad or relish will keep for a long time.

2 eggplants
1 tablespoon seasoned salt
¾ cup olive oil
28 ounces Italian canned tomatoes, cut up (use the juice too)
3 stalks celery, diced
⅓ cup sliced black olives
⅓ cup sliced green olives
2 tablespoons capers, rinsed and drained
¼ cup pine nuts, slightly browned
2 tablespoons red wine vinegar
1 tablespoon sugar
½ teaspoon freshly ground black pepper

Dice the eggplant (skin on) into 1½- to 2-inch cubes and sprinkle with 1 tablespoon salt. Let stand 30 minutes. Drain. Heat half the oil in a skillet and lightly brown the eggplant in it over a high flame. Leave the eggplant a little firm.

In a saucepan, heat the remaining oil, and sauté the celery until it begins to soften, 10–12 minutes. Add the tomatoes, and sauté another 3–5 minutes. Add olives, capers, pine nuts, vinegar, sugar and pepper, and simmer for 12 minutes. Add the browned eggplant and simmer for 15 minutes more. Correct seasoning (taste should be slightly sweet-sour). Chill in refrigerator for at least 4 hours before serving. The longer it refrigerates, the better it gets. If kept refrigerated and tossed every now and then, it will last up to 3 weeks. Makes about 2 quarts.

Pepper Salad

2 red and 2 yellow sweet peppers
Italian extra virgin olive oil
Juice of 1–2 lemons
Seasoned salt and freshly ground black pepper
8 anchovy fillets
Chopped fresh mint
2 teaspoons capers, rinsed and drained (optional)

Roast red and yellow peppers over an open flame or under a broiler until skin blisters and is charred on all sides and both ends. Immediately place in a large paper bag with the top twisted closed. Let "rest" for 20 minutes.

Remove peppers from bag and peel away charred skin. Cut peppers in half lengthwise and remove stems, seeds and ribs. Overlap red and yellow pepper slices and top with extra virgin olive oil and lemon juice, salt and pepper. Chill thoroughly and top each serving with capers, 2 anchovies and chopped fresh mint. Serves 4.

Mushroom and Celery Salad

4 anchovies, mashed, or *1 teaspoon anchovy paste*
1 clove garlic, crushed
Juice of 2 large lemons
½ cup Italian extra virgin olive oil, or to taste
Black pepper
½ pound fresh mushrooms (brown, shiitake, or mushrooms of choice)
2 large celery stalks, strings removed, cut into ⅛-inch slices
¼ cup grated Romano cheese
4 radicchio leaves

To prepare dressing: Whisk together anchovy, garlic and lemon juice in a bowl. Gradually whisk in olive oil. Season to taste with a good dash of freshly ground black pepper and reserve. Clean mushrooms, slice into quarters and place in salad bowl with celery. Sprinkle this with the grated cheese. Toss salad well with the dressing and serve each portion on a radicchio leaf. Serves 4.

Fagiolini Salad

This salad keeps very well and can be prepared a day or two ahead of time. Other ingredients of choice may be added, such as cherry tomatoes, mushrooms, pine nuts or celery.

2 pounds fresh green beans, trimmed
½ cup lemon juice
3 tablespoons red wine vinegar
2 cloves garlic, crushed
1 cup olive oil
Seasoned salt and freshly ground black pepper
1 small red onion, diced or thinly sliced
3 tablespoons grated Romano cheese
⅓ cup julienned sun-dried tomato for garnish

Cook fagiolini (green beans) in boiling salted water until *al dente* (cooked but firm), about 12 minutes for large beans and 8–9 minutes for small beans. Refresh in ice water immediately after straining, then pat dry with towel and refrigerate until needed.

To prepare dressing: In a bowl, combine lemon juice, vinegar and garlic. Slowly whisk in olive oil and a pinch of salt and pepper to taste. Whisk well and reserve.

Place beans and onions in a salad bowl and toss. Season with salt and pepper and toss again. Whisk salad dressing and pour over beans as needed. Toss the beans again and let sit for 10 minutes; toss again. Serve on plate with grated cheese and sun-dried tomatoes on top. Serves 6.

Italian Homestyle Salad

1 head romaine lettuce
8 large fresh sweet basil leaves
1 cucumber
2 large stalks celery, strings removed, cut into 1/3-inch pieces
2 ounces provolone cheese, cut into 1/4-inch julienne
2 medium, very ripe tomatoes, quartered
1/2 cup ceci beans (chickpeas), rinsed and drained
Salt and pepper to taste
1/3 cup Italian extra virgin olive oil
2 tablespoons red wine vinegar
Juice of 1 lemon

In a prechilled salad bowl, break the romaine into small pieces. If the basil leaves are large, tear in half, otherwise leave whole and add to the romaine. Peel the cucumber, cut in half lengthwise, remove seeds, slice thinly, and add to the bowl. Add all other vegetables and the cheese, and toss. Season with salt and pepper and toss again. Prepare dressing by whisking together the olive oil, vinegar and lemon juice. Pour over salad, correct seasonings and toss well. Serve immediately. Serves 6.

Escarole Salad

Slightly bitter, a true salad lover's simple but delicious salad.

1 head escarole
6–8 leaves fresh sweet basil, torn in thirds

6 tablespoons Italian extra virgin olive oil
Juice of 1 lemon
2 tablespoons red wine vinegar
Seasoned salt
Freshly ground black pepper

Discard outside leaves of escarole and wash thoroughly. Cut into 1- to 1½-inch pieces. Drain. Place escarole in salad bowl. Add sweet basil to salad bowl and toss. In a separate bowl mix well the olive oil, lemon juice, vinegar, salt and pepper. Pour over salad and toss, mixing well. Serves 4–6.

Dill Vinaigrette

A snappy dressing for your favorite salad greens.

2 tablespoons grated red onion
6 tablespoons olive oil
3 tablespoons wine vinegar
1 teaspoon Dijon mustard
½ teaspoon Worcestershire sauce
Salt and freshly ground black pepper to taste
1 tablespoon chopped fresh dill (or more if desired)
1 tablespoon chopped fresh parsley
Juice of 1 lemon
Pinch of sugar

Whisk together all ingredients and adjust seasonings.

Squid Salad

2 pounds small squid
Seasoned salt
2 cloves garlic, minced
1 tablespoon fresh mint, chopped
5 tablespoons Italian extra virgin olive oil
Juice of 1 large lemon
1 tablespoon red wine vinegar
Freshly ground black pepper

Clean squid and cut into small pieces (rings), leaving tentacles whole. Boil in 2 quarts water for about 30 minutes or until tender. Drain the squid well and salt them. Blend the other ingredients well and pour over the squid. Marinate, covered, in the refrigerator for several hours, stirring occasionally. Serve cold on radicchio leaves. Serves 4–6.

Tomatoes, Peppers and Mozzarella Di Bufala

4 red sweet peppers
6 firm but ripe tomatoes
12 1/4-inch slices fresh mozzarella di bufala cheese
2 tablespoons lemon juice
2 tablespoons red wine vinegar
1 small clove garlic, minced
Pinch oregano
Olive oil
Seasoned salt and freshly ground black pepper
Capers (optional)

Put the peppers under a hot broiler and roast them, turning occasionally, until the skin is charred black. Cool and skin them. Remove seeds and membranes and halve peppers lengthwise. Skin the tomatoes and slice them into about ¼- to ½-inch thick slices. On a chilled plate, overlap slices of tomato, mozzarella di bufala and pepper, topping with another slice of tomato. You may sprinkle a few rinsed and dried capers over each salad if desired.

For the dressing: Whisk together well the lemon juice, vinegar, garlic, oregano, olive oil and salt and pepper. Whisk again and pour over the chilled salads and serve immediately. Serves 6.

Cold Potato Salad Piranio

An excellent summer side dish.

4 large boiled potatoes, chilled, with skins on
1 tablespoon chopped fresh parsley or mint
6 tablespoons Italian extra virgin olive oil
3 tablespoons red wine vinegar
Seasoned salt and freshly ground black pepper

Cut potatoes into small cubes (about ½ to ¾ inch). Put in salad bowl and sprinkle parsley over them. Blend oil and vinegar separately, add to potatoes and toss lightly. Season with salt and pepper. Thoroughly chill in the refrigerator for at least an hour. Toss lightly and serve. Serves 4.

Orange Salad

This is a delightful, summery salad that goes with almost anything, but especially with duck, fowl or roast meats. Tony says, "Give it a chance. It will surprise you."

4 sweet, seedless oranges
1 teaspoon freshly ground black pepper
¼ cup Italian extra virgin olive oil
Fresh mint, chopped

Peel the oranges and slice into thin wheels. Arrange slices in a circle on each of 4 cold salad plates. Sprinkle with the pepper and oil. Let stand 30 minutes or more. Just before serving, sprinkle generously with mint.

Cranberry Melon Mold

Delicious for a summer buffet.

5 cups cranberry juice cocktail
3 envelopes unflavored gelatin
1 cup dry red wine
1½ cups fresh melon balls (cantaloupe, honeydew, etc.)
Additional melon balls for garnish

Pour 2 cups of the cranberry juice into a saucepan. Sprinkle the gelatin into the juice and allow to stand for 5 minutes, stirring occasionally. Place over low heat and stir constantly until gelatin dissolves. Remove from heat. Stir in the remaining 3 cups cranberry juice cocktail and the wine. Chill until slightly thickened, stirring several times. Fold in melon balls. Turn into a 2-quart mold. Refrigerate until set and firm, at least 3 hours.

To unmold, dip mold in lukewarm water to the depth of the mold, careful not to get any water in it. Place serving dish on top of mold and turn upside down. Give a shake if necessary. Garnish with melon balls all around. Serves 10–12.

Variation: For a crunchy alternative, add some walnut pieces when adding the melon.

Holiday Cranberry Mold

3 packages gelatin dessert mix, 2 strawberry and 1 raspberry
3 cups very hot water
3 cans cranberry sauce (or make your own)
2 packages unflavored gelatin dissolved in ½ the amount of water called for
1 large can crushed pineapple
1 large green apple, peeled and grated
¾ cup fresh orange juice
2 tablespoons lemon juice
1 cup chopped walnuts

Dissolve flavored gelatin mixes in hot water. Mash the cranberry sauce well and add to gelatin mixture. Mix well and add the unflavored gelatin dissolved in cold water. Drain pineapple and add it and the grated apple, stirring well. Then, stirring all the while, add orange juice, lemon juice and nuts. Put in bowl or large mold, stir again and refrigerate until set (very firm), at least 2–3 hours. Unmold before serving (see preceding recipe for directions). Serves a crowd.

Soups

Do you have a kinder, more adaptable friend
in the food world than soup? Who soothes you when
you are ill? Who refuses to leave you when you
are impoverished and stretches its resources to give
you a hearty sustenance and cheer? . . . Soup
is sensitive. You don't catch steak hanging
around when you're poor and sick, do you?

JUDITH MARTIN
(Miss Manners)

UNDER THE CONSTITUTION, a man or woman may not become President of the United States until he or she has reached the age of thirty-five. On the age at which either may become a gourmet the Constitution is silent, but one seldom becomes a gourmet before thirty-five, and usually not until later. As Julian Street wrote: ". . . it takes not only taste but time to gather a rounded knowledge of these matters, for which reason young gourmets have never been as numerous as middle-aged or elderly gourmets."

It is soups and sauces which most command a gourmet's respect—or rejection. Few other foods are so lucid in revealing at once a cook's art, or the lack of it. "The soul of any kitchen," Tony has said, "is the soups and sauces." (As an amateur, a diner rather than a cook, I would add the omelet to Tony's duo, for a light and graceful omelet has become a regrettably vestigial dish, at least in America.)

SOUPS

Soup, *Larousse Gastronomique* says, must be in perfect harmony with the whole meal. Some of us could live on soups, one of the most widely favored forms of food, clear or otherwise, but especially otherwise. And Tony has an Italianate genius for soups, of which his versions are sometimes suitable for main courses. "The richer the stock, the richer the flavor of the soup," Tony says.

. . . Who soothes you when you are ill?

Shellfish Soup Nonna

This is a very hearty main-course soup. Add a crusty loaf of Italian or French bread and it's a whole meal.

48 mussels, scrubbed and with beards removed
48 clams (steamers, if desired)
1½ pounds shrimp, shelled and deveined
1 pound squid
¾ pound scallops
1 cup Italian olive oil
1 large onion, chopped
1½ pounds tomatoes, peeled, seeded, drained and chopped
8 cloves garlic, crushed in a garlic press
1 teaspoon oregano
1–2 teaspoons fennel seeds
1 level teaspoon crushed red pepper
Seasoned salt and freshly ground black pepper
1 cup dry white vermouth or white wine
2 quarts fish stock
2 tablespoons chopped fresh parsley
12 slices French or Italian bread, crusts removed, sautéed in olive oil

Cut the squid into strips, leaving the tentacles whole. Put ¼ cup of the olive oil with the mussels and clams in a tightly covered pot and shake the pot over high heat until the shells open. Pour the shellfish and their liquid into a colander placed over a bowl. Remove the clams and mussels from their shells and allow their liquid to drain into the bowl. Strain the liquid through several thicknesses of cheesecloth. Keep the mussels and clams warm in a covered bowl.

Heat the remaining oil in a large thick pot over medium heat. Add the onion and cook until golden. Add the squid and the shellfish liquid. Cover the pot and cook for 10 minutes. Add the tomatoes, garlic, oregano, fennel seeds, red pepper flakes, seasoned salt, black pepper and white wine. Cook another 7 minutes.

Add the scallops, shrimp and fish stock. Bring to a boil. Reduce the heat and simmer for 12 minutes. Just before removing from the fire, add the parsley, mussels and clams. Arrange sautéed slices of French or Italian bread in individual soup bowls. Spoon a selection of the shellfish on each piece of toast. Correct the seasoning of the broth and ladle a little broth into each bowl. Serves 6–8 hungry people.

Shrimp Bisque

1 pound fresh shrimp, cooked, shelled, deveined and minced
1 cup half-and-half
2 tablespoons butter
1 small onion, minced
2 stalks celery, minced
1 tablespoon flour
1 teaspoon seasoned salt
½ teaspoon paprika
Generous dash freshly ground white pepper
2 cups milk
1 cup heavy cream
3 tablespoons good dry sherry
Additional cooked shrimp for garnish

Purée shrimp in blender with half-and-half and set aside. Melt butter in skillet and sauté the onion and celery over moderate heat for about 7–8 minutes, or until cooked. Blend in flour, salt, paprika and pepper, stirring well. Add shrimp purée, milk and cream. Simmer, stirring constantly until slightly thickened. Stir in sherry before serving. Garnish each cup or bowl with shrimp halves or pieces. Serves 6.

Oyster Bisque

1 pint oysters
4 cups light cream
1 slice onion
2 stalks celery
1 sprig parsley
Piece bay leaf
1/3 cup butter
1/3 cup flour
Salt and pepper to taste

Drain oysters and chop. Heat slowly to the boiling point and press through a coarse sieve.

Scald cream with onion, celery, parsley and bay leaf. Melt butter, stir in flour, and strain cream into butter-flour mixture. Stir over a low fire or hot water until mixture thickens. Add the strained oysters and season with salt and pepper to taste.

If a thinner soup is desired, milk may be substituted for the light cream. Serve hot with freshly made croutons. Serves 4.

Oysters Rockefeller Soup

5 tablespoons butter
5 tablespoons flour
3–4 cloves garlic
1 bunch scallions
3 cups oysters, minced and drained
1½ cups chicken stock
3 cups heavy cream, scalded
20 ounces frozen, chopped spinach, cooked and drained
Seasoned salt, cayenne, Tabasco and nutmeg to taste

Melt butter and stir in flour. Add garlic and scallions. Cook over medium-high heat until scallions are transparent. Add oysters. Cook until oysters are slightly firm. Add chicken stock and cream. Stir well to combine.

Add spinach and bring to a boil. Remove soup from heat and allow to cool a bit. Process in a blender or food processor until well blended. Return to heat and add seasonings. Serves 6.

Note: For a wonderful extra touch, add ½ ounce each green crème de menthe and Sambuca to the finished soup and let it simmer a minute.

Cream of Mussels Soup

2 shallots, minced
2 cups dry white wine
36 mussels in shells, cleaned
1 small red onion, chopped
1 leek, white part only, halved lengthwise and chopped
1 rib of celery, chopped
½ fennel bulb, chopped
4 cloves garlic, minced
¼ teaspoon crumbled saffron threads
1 stick butter
8 cups fish stock
2 cups heavy cream
Salt and pepper
4 tablespoons cornstarch, dissolved in ¼ cup cold water

In a large saucepan, combine the shallots, 1 cup wine and the mussels. Bring the wine to a boil and steam the mussels, covered (shaking the pan often) for 3–4 minutes, or until shells open. Transfer the mussels to a bowl, discarding any unopened ones. Remove mussels from shells; discard the shells. Strain the cooking liquid through a fine sieve and reserve.

In a kettle, cook the onion, leek, celery, fennel, garlic and saffron in butter over low heat, stirring until vegetables are tender. Add the remaining 1 cup of wine, the reserved cooking liquid, the stock and half the mussels. Bring the liquid to a boil, add the cream and cook the mixture at a low boil, stirring for 30 minutes. In a blender or food processor purée the mixture in batches and return the purée to the kettle. Season with salt and pepper and bring to a boil. Whisk the cornstarch mixture and add it to the purée, whisking. Simmer soup for 3 minutes. Ladle into heated bowls and garnish with the remaining mussels. Serves 8–10.

Lentil Soup

"When I was a boy," Tony says, "we knew cold weather was coming when we smelled lentils on the stove."

12–13 cups chicken stock
2 large onions, chopped fine
2 carrots, chopped fine
2 cups minced celery
1 medium tomato, peeled and chopped fine
Ham bone with a good chunk of meat on it
2 cups dried lentils
4 cloves garlic, chopped fine
Seasoned salt
Freshly ground black pepper
2 tablespoons wine vinegar (optional)

In a large saucepan, combine stock, onions, carrots, celery, tomato and ham bone. Cover and simmer for 1 hour. Remove the ham bone and set aside.

Add lentils, cover and simmer 40 minutes. Remove the meat from ham bone and cut into chunks. Add ham, garlic and vinegar, and simmer 10–15 minutes. Season to taste with seasoned salt and a good pinch of pepper. Serves a crowd.

Black Bean Soup

4 cups black beans, washed
Cold water as needed
3 stalks celery
3 large onions, finely chopped
½ cup butter
2½ tablespoons flour
½ cup finely chopped parsley
Rind and bone of 1 cooked smoked ham
3 leeks, thinly sliced
4 bay leaves
1 tablespoon seasoned salt
1 teaspoon freshly ground black pepper
1 cup dry Madeira wine
Pinch of cayenne pepper
Croutons or sour cream (optional)

Soak the beans overnight in enough cold water to cover them, then drain. Add 5 quarts cold water and cook the beans over low heat for 1½ hours.

In a soup kettle over low heat, sauté the celery and onions in butter for about 6–8 minutes or until tender. Blend in flour and chopped parsley and cook the mixture, stirring 1 minute.

Gradually stir in the beans and their water. Add the rind and the bone of the ham (rind should be chopped in small pieces), leeks, bay leaves, seasoned salt and pepper. Simmer the soup for 4 hours.

Remove and discard the ham bone and bay leaves. Force the remainder through a sieve. Mix the puréed beans with their broth and add the Madeira and cayenne. Heat and stir the soup and serve immediately with croutons or a dollop of sour cream. Serves 10–12.

Red Bean Soup

1 cup chopped onion
1 cup chopped carrot
4 cloves garlic, minced
1 stalk celery, chopped
3 tablespoons olive oil
6 cups water
1½ cups dried red kidney beans, rinsed
1 meaty ham bone
36 ounces canned Italian tomatoes
1 tablespoon tomato paste
Salt and black pepper
Pinch of oregano
½ cup freshly grated Parmesan cheese

In a large saucepan cook the onion, carrot, garlic and celery in the oil over a moderately low heat, stirring, for 5 minutes or until vegetables are softened. Add the water, beans and ham bone. Bring to a boil and simmer partially covered for about an hour or until beans are barely tender.

Add the tomatoes, tomato paste, salt and pepper to taste, and a pinch of oregano. Simmer the soup, breaking up the tomatoes with a spoon, for about 45 minutes more, or until the beans are very soft.

Remove the ham bone but return meat to the soup. Purée the soup in a blender or food processor and return to the saucepan. Correct seasonings. Serve hot with freshly grated Parmesan cheese on the side. Serves 6.

Minestrone

"This is a hearty, main-course soup with a thousand versions, at least," says Tony. "This is an excellent one."

1 cup dried cannellini or white beans
1 cup dried kidney beans
1 cup dried Roman, pinto, black or other beans of choice
4 quarts water
Ham bone (or prosciutto bone) with a little meat on it
3–4 tablespoons Italian olive oil
1 cup chopped onions
2–3 carrots, diced
2–3 stalks celery, sliced
3 cups diced zucchini
2 cups peeled and chopped tomatoes
4 cups shredded cabbage
6 chicken bouillon cubes
4 cloves garlic, minced
1 tablespoon seasoned salt
1½-2 teaspoons freshly ground black pepper
4 tablespoons minced parsley
¾ cup grated Parmesan
Small pasta, cooked

Wash the beans, cover with water, and bring to a boil. Remove from heat and let soak 1 hour. Drain and add 4 quarts of water. Bring to a boil and cook over low heat 1½ hours. After 1 hour, add the ham bone.

Meanwhile, prepare the vegetables: In a skillet add the oil and onions. Sauté about 5 minutes. Mix in the carrots, celery and zucchini; sauté 5 minutes, stirring frequently. Add to the cooked beans. Add the tomatoes, cabbage, bouillon cubes, garlic, salt and pepper. Cook over low heat 1¼ hours. Mix in parsley and cook another 15 minutes. Just before serving, stir in the cheese and add a little cooked pasta (any small pasta). Serve with additional grated cheese. Serves 10–12.

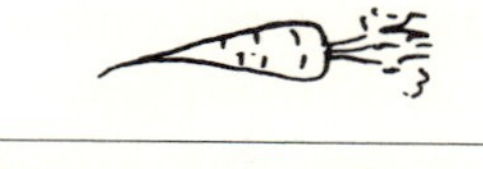

Minestrone Magra

Tony: "My grandmother always said that a good minestrone has to have at least three kinds of beans in it. This is a good meatless version."

½ pound dried red beans
½ pound dried cannellini or Great Northern white beans
½ cup olive oil
2 medium carrots, cut into ¼-inch dice
1 medium red onion, cut into ¼-inch dice
2 medium celery ribs, cut into ¼-inch dice
½ pound mushrooms, cut into ¼-inch dice
½ small head Savoy cabbage, shredded
1 28-ounce can Italian tomatoes (juice and all), chopped
8 cups boiling chicken stock
¼ pound lentils, rinsed and drained
1 19-ounce can ceci or chickpeas, drained and rinsed
½ pound tubetti or other short pasta
Seasoned salt to taste
1 teaspoon freshly ground black pepper
2 large cloves garlic, crushed (optional)
4 ounces freshly grated Romano or Parmesan cheese

Place the red and cannellini beans in a large bowl and soak overnight in enough cold water to cover by 2 inches; drain. Or place the beans in a large saucepan, add water to cover and bring to a boil over high heat. Boil for 2 minutes, then remove from heat and let the beans soak, covered, for 1 hour; drain.

In a stockpot or large flameproof casserole, heat the olive oil over moderate heat. Add the carrots, onion and celery and cook until the vegetables are softened but not browned, 10–12 minutes. Add the mushrooms and cook until they lose their juices and begin to brown, about 10 minutes. Add the cabbage and cook until wilted, about 5 minutes. Add the tomatoes and cook for 5 minutes. Add the drained red and cannellini beans and the boiling chicken broth. Simmer over moderately low heat, partially covered, for 45 minutes.

Add the lentils to the soup and cook, partially covered, until the beans are tender, 1–1½ hours. (If the soup becomes too thick, add 1–3 cups of hot chicken broth.)

Add the chickpeas, pasta, salt, pepper and garlic. Cook the pasta to the *al dente* stage. Serve hot with a generous sprinkling of grated cheese. Pass the remaining cheese separately. Serves 8–10.

Creamy Garden Bisque

Any combination of vegetables can be used in this soup.

¼ cup unsalted butter
2 large onions, chopped
2 stalks celery, chopped
1 large carrot, peeled and chopped
Stems from 1 bunch of parsley
4 cloves garlic, minced
1½ teaspoons dried thyme, crumbled
1 quart chicken stock
1 teaspoon seasoned salt

3 ears corn, husked
3 large carrots, peeled
1 large sweet red pepper
1 medium zucchini
2 tomatoes, seeded
¼ pound green beans, trimmed and cut in ⅓-inch pieces
⅓ cup whipping cream
Freshly ground white pepper (be generous)
¼ cup minced fresh herbs (basil, parsley, marjoram, thyme)

Melt butter in heavy medium saucepan over medium heat. Stir in next 6 ingredients. Cover and cook until vegetables are light brown, stirring occasionally, about 15–20 minutes.

Stir in the stock and salt and bring to a boil. Reduce heat, cover partially and simmer until vegetables are very tender, about 30 minutes. Strain soup and return to pan. Scrape corn into a bowl, using knife. Cut carrots, red pepper, zucchini and tomatoes into ⅓-inch pieces.

Bring soup to boil, add carrots and boil 5 minutes. Add green beans and red peppers and boil 5 minutes. Add zucchini and boil 5 minutes. Add tomatoes and corn and bring to a simmer. Stir in cream and pepper. Adjust seasonings. Sprinkle with herbs and serve hot. Add a tablespoon of dry sherry to each serving for a marvelous touch. Serves 6–8.

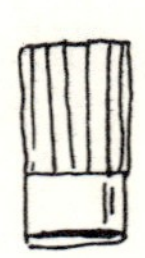

Cauliflower Soup with Pesto

Pesto:

2 cups (packed) fresh basil leaves
2 tablespoons pine nuts
2–3 cloves garlic
½ cup Italian olive oil
1 teaspoon seasoned salt
3 tablespoons freshly grated Parmesan
3 tablespoons freshly grated Romano
3 tablespoons butter (at room temperature)
½ teaspoon freshly ground black pepper

Soup:

3 leeks, sliced (white part only)
1 large cauliflower, separated into florets
1 potato, peeled, boiled and thinly sliced
6 cups chicken stock, preferably homemade
Seasoned salt
Freshly ground white pepper

For pesto: Purée basil, pine nuts and garlic with olive oil and salt in a blender or processor. Transfer to a bowl and beat in cheeses, butter and pepper.

For soup: Combine vegetables and stock in a large saucepan and bring to a boil. Reduce heat and simmer until vegetables are tender. Cool slightly. Purée in blender. Season with salt and a good pinch of pepper. (This soup can be prepared in advance and refrigerated until needed.) To serve, gently reheat soup. Ladle into bowls. Swirl 1½ tablespoons of pesto into each bowl. Serves 8.

Tomato-Potato Soup with Aioli

2 tablespoons unsalted butter
1 tablespoon olive oil
1 cup finely chopped onion
1 cup coarsely chopped leeks (white part only)
1 tablespoon minced garlic
Cayenne pepper
3 cups water
1 28-ounce can tomatoes, drained and coarsely chopped
½ teaspoon sugar
1½ pounds potatoes, peeled and coarsely chopped
2 teaspoons tomato paste
1 teaspoon salt
½ teaspoon pepper
Aioli (see recipe, page 87)

Melt butter with oil in large heavy saucepan over high heat. Add onion, leeks, garlic and cayenne, and sauté for 20 seconds. Mix in water, tomatoes and sugar, and bring to a boil. Reduce heat, cover and simmer 15 minutes.

Stir in potatoes, tomato paste and salt. Cover saucepan and simmer soup until potatoes are tender, stirring occasionally, about 40 minutes.

Purée soup in processor or blender until smooth. Return soup to pan, stir in pepper to taste and adjust seasonings. Reheat soup. Ladle into bowls and top with a dollop of aioli. Serves 8.

Eggplant Soup

½ cup Great Northern white, navy, or cannellini beans
4 cups water
2 cups mixed chopped onions and white of leeks
3 tablespoons corn oil
2 bay leaves
½ teaspoon grated black pepper or lightly crushed peppercorns
½ teaspoon crumbled dried thyme
Chopped fresh parsley and/or chives
Crumbled basil, oregano, or *crushed fennel seed*
½ pound Italian sausage, sliced (optional)
1 eggplant (weight approximately 1 pound), peeled, diced and tossed with 4 teaspoons salt
Olive oil for sautéing
1 pound ripe tomatoes, peeled, seeded and chopped
4 cloves garlic, minced
4 cups chicken stock or as needed
½ cup freshly grated Parmesan cheese

Combine beans and water, and bring to a rapid boil for 2 minutes. Cover, remove from heat and let stand for 1 hour.

Sauté onions and leeks slowly in corn oil, raise heat and brown lightly. Add to the beans along with seasonings and herbs. Bring to a simmer, cover with tilted lid and simmer for 1½ hours, or until beans are just tender. Bake sausage slices at 350° for 20 minutes. Drain and set aside.

Place salted eggplant in a colander and drain for 20 minutes, reserving liquid. Sauté eggplant in olive oil until lightly browned. Add tomatoes, garlic, stock and reserved eggplant liquid. Simmer, covered, for 15 minutes, then combine with the beans. Add sausage and cook slowly, uncovered, for 15 minutes. Add more herbs if necessary and check salt and pepper. Serve with Parmesan cheese on the side. Serves 8.

Note: The sausage may be omitted, making the soup meatless but nevertheless delicious.

Pumpkin Soup

Simple, surprising and delicious.

4 cups peeled and cubed pumpkin
1/8 teaspoon ground allspice
1/8 teaspoon cinnamon
4 cups chicken stock or broth
Seasoned salt
Freshly ground white pepper
2 tablespoons butter
2 leeks, sliced
Whipped cream or sour cream

In a large heavy saucepan, bring the pumpkin, spices and stock to a boil over high heat. Lower heat, cover and simmer for 30 minutes or until the squash is tender. Purée in a food processor or blender. Salt and pepper to taste (this soup should be a little spicy).

In a separate saucepan, melt the butter over medium heat. Sauté the leeks until golden, about 6–8 minutes. Stir in the pumpkin purée and heat for several minutes, stirring. If the soup is too thick, thin it with additional stock and correct seasoning. Serve very hot with a dollop of whipped cream or sour cream on top and a pinch of allspice over the cream. Serves 6.

Cream of Asparagus and Leek Soup

3 cups chopped asparagus
3 cups leeks
1 teaspoon tarragon
1 tablespoon chopped parsley
4 cups chicken stock
1½–2 cups heavy cream
2–3 tablespoons medium sherry
Seasoned salt
Freshly ground white pepper
Asparagus tips for garnish

Put the asparagus, leeks, tarragon, parsley and stock in a saucepan and bring to a boil over high heat. Lower the heat and simmer partially covered for 10–15 minutes or until vegetables are tender.

In a food processor or blender, purée the soup until a fine consistency. Return the purée to the saucepan and stir in the cream and sherry. (To serve cold, chill for 3–4 hours, then add the cream and sherry.) Keep stirring and simmering over medium heat until soup is very hot and of nice consistency. Add seasoned salt and white pepper to taste. An extra pinch of pepper enhances the soup. Garnish with asparagus tips. Serves 6.

Cream of Fennel Soup

This fine soup draws its distinctive flavor from the bulbous root of the fennel plant, a relative of parsley and cilantro. It is used both as a flavoring and as a vegetable. Fresh fennel is a large white bulb with pale green feathery leaves. The bulb should be snow white and firm when you buy it. An excellent source of Vitamin A, it is also low in calories.

5 tablespoons unsalted butter
½ cup chopped onion
2½ cups chopped fennel
1 cup heavy cream
1 cup chicken or veal stock
Watercress leaves
Freshly ground pepper

Heat butter in a 2-quart sauce pot. Add onions and fennel. Cover and cook about 12 minutes over medium flame.

Add cream to mixture and purée. Return purée mixture to the pot and stir in stock. Cook over medium flame just until heated (do not boil). Garnish with the watercress leaves and freshly ground pepper. Serves 4.

Watercress Soup

3 medium leeks, diced
1½ pounds zucchini, peeled and coarsely chopped
2 tablespoons unsalted butter
4 cups chicken stock
1 bunch watercress, chopped
2–4 tablespoons heavy cream
Salt and pepper

Heat butter in a 4-quart pot. Add leeks and cook until soft. Add zucchini and sauté for 3 minutes without browning. Add stock and simmer uncovered until zucchini is tender. Season with salt and pepper. Bring soup to a boil and add the watercress. Simmer for 2 to 3 minutes, then blend until smooth in a food processor. Add the cream just before serving. (Sour cream may be used if you prefer.) Soup may be served hot or cold. Serves 6.

Cold Tomato, Basil and Walnut Soup

An excellent, summery soup.

3 pounds fresh ripe tomatoes, peeled, cored and seeded or 2 28-ounce cans Italian plum tomatoes, drained
1/3 cup minced fresh basil
2 tablespoons walnut oil
1 teaspoon honey
1 tablespoon balsamic vinegar
1 teaspoon salt
Freshly ground pepper
1/2 cup toasted walnuts, chopped
Small basil sprigs

Purée half the tomatoes in processor. Transfer to glass or ceramic bowl. Do not use metal. Repeat with the remaining tomatoes. Add all remaining ingredients to tomatoes except walnuts and basil sprigs. Mix to blend. Adjust seasonings. Cover and refrigerate at least 3 hours. (This can be prepared a day ahead.) Garnish with the walnuts and basil sprigs. Serves 6.

Chilled Borsch

Borsch is frequently requested for parties in the wine cellar.

1 cup sour cream
1 can (16 ounces) cut or sliced beets
3 beef bouillon cubes dissolved in 1/4 cup boiling water
2 tablespoons dark brown sugar
1 3/4 cups cold water

2 tablespoons fresh lemon juice
1/2 teaspoon salt
1/4 teaspoon ground white pepper
2 tablespoons minced scallions, green tops included

Place the sour cream in a tall refrigerator container. Drain beets, reserving the liquid, and dice the beets. Gradually stir beet liquid into the sour cream. Add beets and remaining ingredients, mixing very well. Cover and refrigerate for 8 hours or more—overnight is best. Serve well-chilled and mix well just before serving. Serves 6.

Velvety Roquefort Vichyssoise

1 cup finely chopped leeks (white part only)
1/2 cup finely chopped onion
1/4 cup unsalted butter
1 quart chicken stock
2 cups diced pared potatoes
1/4 teaspoon seasoned salt
Pinch white pepper
1/4 teaspoon minced fresh dill
2 cups buttermilk
3/4 cup Roquefort cheese, crumbled
2 tablespoons chopped chives or scallion tops

Sauté leeks and onion in butter until soft and golden. Stir in stock, potatoes, salt and pepper. Heat to boiling. Reduce heat. Simmer uncovered until potatoes are tender, about 15–20 minutes. Purée soup until smooth, then add dill. Refrigerate covered until very cold, about 4–5 hours.

Stir in buttermilk just before serving, taste and adjust seasoning. Ladle into soup bowls and top with chives and crumbled Roquefort. Serves 6.

Stilton Soup

This soup is wonderful on a cold day.

1½ cups half-and-half
1 bay leaf
¼ cup sliced onion
2 tablespoons butter
2 tablespoons flour
2 cups chicken stock
5 ounces crumbled Stilton cheese
Seasoned salt
Freshly ground white pepper
Dry sherry (optional)

Bring the half-and-half, bay leaf and onion to a boil. Remove from heat, cover and leave for 10 minutes. Strain.

Melt the butter in a large saucepan, stir in the flour and cook stirring over low to moderate heat for 1½–2 minutes. Remove the pan from the heat and pour in the half-and-half, stirring constantly. Return the pan to the heat and cook for 1 minute, stirring constantly. Then add the stock, stir well, bring the soup to a boil, and let it simmer 5 minutes.

Remove pan from heat and immediately add cheese. Stir until the cheese melts, then season to taste with salt and pepper. Serve hot with a good crusty bread. A teaspoon or more of dry sherry may be added to each serving. Serves 4.

Sauces

The best sauce in the world is hunger.
MIGUEL DE CERVANTES

A SAUCE, *Larousse* says, is simply a liquid seasoning for food—to which Tony adds, "One that enhances, not conceals or masks, flavor." One feels a warm, homey comfort in the instruction of an old woman who was giving a friend one of her prized recipes—a pinch of this, a dab of that, she said, "and four gurgles of syrup." Making most of these sauces is, of course, more disciplined than that. As Tony has said of the sauces (and some other recipes), a good cook "must have a clock in his head."

The great French chef Fernand Point once said, "What is a béarnaise sauce? An egg yolk, some shallots, some tarragon. But believe me, it requires years of practice for the result to be perfect. Take your eyes off it for an instant and it will be unusable." To this wisdom, Tony added one suggestion instantly: "I think the chef would also include a drop of demiglace."

Spicy Marinara

You'll never taste a better marinara than this one.

⅓ cup Italian extra virgin olive oil
4 garlic cloves, chopped fine
½ cup dry white or red wine
½ teaspoon crushed red pepper (or more if desired)
20 ounces ripe tomatoes, peeled, seeded and chopped, or *1 28-ounce can of imported Italian tomatoes (these* must *be top-quality)*
Pinch of seasoned salt
Pinch of sugar
2 tablespoons chopped fresh basil

In a heavy saucepan, heat the olive oil over medium heat. Sauté garlic until it begins to color slightly. Pour in wine and cook until a good bit of the liquid evaporates. Add the crushed red pepper, tomatoes, salt and sugar and cook over low heat for 20 minutes, until sauce thickens slightly. Add the basil and cook 5 minutes more. Makes about 2½ cups or enough sauce for 1 pound of pasta.

Note: Omit the red pepper for a milder marinara.

Salsa Verde

This classic Italian green sauce is served with boiled meats or fried seafood. ("It's the Italian *pico de gallo*," says Tony.)

6 anchovy fillets
½ cup chopped parsley
¼–½ cup chopped fresh sweet basil
1 medium potato, boiled, peeled and mashed

3/4 teaspoon finely minced garlic
2 tablespoons grated yellow onion
1/2 teaspoon seasoned salt (or to taste)
1/2 teaspoon freshly ground black pepper
Pinch of cayenne
7 tablespoons Italian extra virgin oil
2 tablespoons white vinegar
2 tablespoons lemon juice

Mix together the anchovy, parsley, basil, potato, garlic, onion, salt and both peppers. (The onion may be omitted if desired.) Stir thoroughly, until mixture becomes pasty in consistency. Add olive oil, 1 tablespoon at a time, whisking constantly, then add vinegar and lemon juice and correct seasonings, whisking all the time. Makes 2½–3 cups.

Aioli

Aioli is a garlic mayonnaise that enhances fried or boiled seafood as well as the Tomato-Potato Soup on page 77.

1 egg, room temperature
1½ teaspoons fresh lemon juice
1 teaspoon minced garlic
1/4 teaspoon seasoned salt
1/3 cup olive oil
1/3 cup vegetable oil
1 tablespoon minced fresh parsley
Tabasco

Blend egg, lemon juice, garlic and salt in processor or blender until smooth. With machine running, slowly add oils through tube. Once mixture begins to thicken, oil can be added more quickly. Stir in parsley, and season with Tabasco to taste.

Mogghiu

Tony: "This is an old Sicilian sauce, excellent over broiled fish, chicken or steak. I like also to baste whatever meat I'm charcoaling with this sauce and then spoon more on top when the meat is finished and garnish with a little more fresh chopped mint over all."

Juice of 1 lemon
½ cup chopped fresh mint, plus more chopped mint as garnish
2–3 teaspoons minced garlic
4 tablespoons Italian extra virgin olive oil
⅓ cup red wine vinegar (or a little more to taste)
1–2 tablespoons water

Whisk all ingredients together in a bowl. Serve at room temperature over meat just after broiling. Serves 4.

Salsa Cruda

An Italian sauce for boiled or broiled meat, fowl or fish. (For another version, see page 116.)

2 cloves garlic, chopped
½ cup chopped scallions
4 tablespoons chopped fresh basil
1 large ripe tomato, coarsely chopped
2 tablespoons wine vinegar
3 tablespoons good Italian olive oil

½ cup chopped arugula
Seasoned salt and freshly ground black pepper to taste
Pinch crushed red pepper flakes

Put all ingredients into a food processor and blend. Serve at room temperature or chilled. Makes about 1½ cups.

Mascarpone Sauce for Tortellini

1 clove garlic, minced
1 tablespoon minced shallots
3 tablespoons butter
1½ cups heavy cream
2 ounces white vermouth
6–7 ounces Mascarpone cheese, broken into small pieces
Pinch of nutmeg, white pepper and salt
2 tablespoons pine nuts, lightly toasted
1 tablespoon basil, chopped (fresh or dried)

Sauté garlic and shallots in butter until shallots are translucent. Add cream and reduce somewhat. Add vermouth and Mascarpone cheese, piece by piece, stirring well. After the cheese is melted and sauce has a nice consistency, add the seasonings, pine nuts and basil. Stir and serve over pasta immediately. Top each plate of pasta with freshly grated pepper. Makes about 2 cups.

Walnut or Pecan Sauce

A rich, garlicky sauce with many uses, especially for seafood and ravioli.

2 ounces chopped walnuts, pecans or both, lightly toasted
3 tablespoons unsalted butter
2 tablespoons freshly grated Parmesan cheese
2 cloves garlic, chopped
½ cup fruity Italian olive oil
¼ cup heavy cream, whipped
Seasoned salt and freshly ground black pepper
Chicken broth
Fresh parsley, chopped (optional)

In a food processor or blender combine nuts, butter, grated cheese and garlic. Process until mixture becomes pasty. With machine running, slowly pour oil through feed tube and process until smooth.

Transfer to a mixing bowl and fold in whipped cream. Season with the seasoned salt and a good pinch of pepper. Refrigerate until needed.

For each serving, stir in 2 tablespoons mixture into ¼ cup chicken broth. Cook over medium heat until sauce thickens slightly. Serve immediately. Sprinkle a little chopped fresh parsley over as a garnish if desired. Makes about 2 cups.

Lime Butter Sauce

A versatile sauce that complements grilled fish, chicken or vegetables. Tony's serves it over sautéed soft-shell crab.

2 tablespoons minced shallot
1½ teaspoons grated lime rind

¼ cup strained fresh lime juice
¼ cup dry white wine
½ cup cold unsalted butter, cut into bits
White pepper to taste
Salt

In a small heavy stainless steel or enameled saucepan, cook the shallots with the lime rind in the lime juice and wine until the liquid is reduced to about 2 tablespoons. Remove pan from heat and add 1 tablespoon cold water. Reduce heat to low and whisk in the butter, 1 piece at a time, lifting the pan from the heat occasionally to cool the mixture and adding each new piece before the previous one has completely melted. (The sauce must not get hot enough to liquefy. It should be the consistency of hollandaise.) The sauce may be strained, if desired. Whisk in the white pepper and salt to taste. Makes about ⅔ cup.

Armagnac Sauce

Excellent for fowl or grilled veal.

2 egg yolks
2 teaspoons Armagnac
2 teaspoons paprika
½ teaspoon Worcestershire sauce
½ teaspoon salt
½ teaspoon white pepper
¾ cup oil
⅓ cup heavy cream, whipped
Pinch of cayenne

Whisk all ingredients, except oil and cream, in bowl until blended. Whisk in oil in a slow, steady stream until sauce is thick and smooth. Fold in cream, adjust seasonings.

Cream Garlic Sauce

Wonderful over grilled shrimp, fish or fowl.

4 tablespoons butter
4 large cloves garlic, chopped very fine
1 tablespoon all-purpose flour
2 egg yolks
1½ cups heavy cream
Pinch seasoned salt
Pinch freshly ground white pepper
Pinch red pepper flakes

Melt the butter in a saucepan. Add the garlic and cook, stirring until it turns golden. (Do not let it brown.) Add the flour and cook, stirring, for about 2½ minutes.

In another bowl, beat the egg yolks, cream and seasonings. Add to the mixture on the stove. Let simmer, stirring constantly for 12–15 minutes, or until desired consistency. Makes about 1⅔ cups.

Garlic Sauce for Fried Seafood

½ pound white bread, crusts trimmed
1 cup cold water
6 cloves garlic
½ teaspoon seasoned salt
½ cup finely ground walnuts
⅓ cup pine nuts, lightly toasted
½ cup Italian olive oil
½ cup white wine vinegar
Warm water

Black pepper
Olives
Mint leaves (optional)

Grind bread to coarse crumbs in a processor. Transfer to a bowl. Add 1 cup cold water and let stand until absorbed, about 3 minutes. Squeeze any excess liquid from crumbs.

Grind garlic and salt to a paste in processor. Add walnuts and pine nuts and grind to a fine consistency. Add bread crumbs and blend until a paste forms. With processor running, slowly add oil and vinegar through the feed tube and blend until smooth. Add enough warm water (about ½ cup) to form a sauce that mounds in a spoon. Add a good pinch of pepper, blend a second more.

Garnish with olives and mint leaves before serving. Sauce can be made in advance, refrigerated and then brought to room temperature before serving. Makes about 2 cups and keeps well in the refrigerator.

Remoulade

2 cups good-quality mayonnaise (or homemade)
2 cloves garlic, minced
1 tablespoon capers, washed, drained and chopped
6 anchovy fillets, drained and mashed
1 teaspoon Worcestershire sauce
¼ – ½ teaspoon cayenne
Juice of 1 lemon
1 tablespoon creole mustard, or to taste
1 tablespoon chili cocktail sauce or ketchup
Dash of Tabasco (optional)

In a bowl, whisk or mix well all of the ingredients and chill covered for at least 1 hour before serving. This will keep in the refrigerator for several days. Makes about 2½ cups.

Sweet Red Pepper Sauce

Excellent with fried or cold boiled seafood.

1½ pounds sweet red peppers
2 tablespoons olive oil
Cayenne
Salt
White pepper

Arrange peppers on broiler rack pan and place under a preheated broiler about 6 inches from the heat, turning them frequently, for 10–15 minutes, or until the skins are blistered and charred.

Put the peppers in a paper bag, close the bag, and let the peppers rest until they are cool enough to handle.

Working over a bowl, remove and discard the skins, stems and seeds from the peppers, reserving any juice.

In a food processor fitted with a steel blade, or in a blender, purée the peppers with the reserved juice. With the motor running, add 2 tablespoons olive oil (or more or less, to taste) and cayenne, salt and white pepper to taste and blend the mixture until it is smooth. Makes about 2 cups.

Red Wine Sauce for Beef or Fowl

8 tablespoons butter
4 tablespoons finely chopped red onion
1 cup red wine or port
1 large clove garlic, peeled and crushed
½ teaspoon thyme
2 tablespoons demiglace

1 teaspoon Dijon mustard
Freshly ground black pepper

Add 1 tablespoon butter and the onion to a hot saucepan. Sauté the onion over low heat for 2–3 minutes, then pour in the red wine. Reduce by about half. Add the garlic, thyme and demiglace and cook 1–2 minutes more. Remove pan from heat and gradually beat in the rest of the butter (cut into small pieces) followed by the mustard. Add freshly ground pepper to taste and serve immediately.

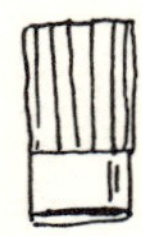

Szechwan Beurre Blanc

A zesty butter sauce that is great with crabmeat, fish or chicken.

2 tablespoons toasted Szechwan peppercorns
1 teaspoon black peppercorns
3/4 cup dry white wine
2 tablespoons minced shallots
1 teaspoon green peppercorns, rinsed, drained and crushed
1 cup unsalted butter, cut into 16 pieces
1/4 teaspoon salt

Crush Szechwan and black peppercorns, using mortar and pestle. Combine with wine, shallots and crushed green peppercorns in a heavy saucepan over high heat. Boil until reduced to 2 tablespoons. Remove pan from heat and reduce heat to low. Whisk 2 pieces of butter into the mixture 1 at a time. Return pan to heat and whisk in remaining butter, one piece at a time, lifting pan from heat if drops of melted butter appear. Whisk in salt and serve immediately.

Orange Beurre Blanc

This is excellent over poached or broiled shrimp, fish or chicken. Orange slices and chopped mint make wonderful garnishes for this sauce.

1 cup plus 2 tablespoons fresh orange juice
1 tablespoon diced orange zest
4 tablespoons white wine vinegar
½ cup white wine
1 tablespoon chopped shallots
3 tablespoons heavy cream
1 cup unsalted butter at room temperature
Seasoned salt to taste
Cayenne pepper to taste

Combine the orange juice, orange zest, vinegar, wine and shallots in a saucepan and bring to a boil. Simmer over medium heat for about 5 minutes, or until the liquid is reduced by half. Lower the heat to medium low. Add the cream and let simmer 2 minutes. Gradually whisk in the butter, about a tablespoon at a time. During this process the heat must be very low so the sauce never simmers. Take the pan off the heat now and then if need be. Add the seasoned salt and cayenne to taste and serve immediately.

Lingonberry Sauce for Duck

Enhances most fowl.

1½ tablespoons raspberry vinegar
3 tablespoons wild ligonberry conserve
2 teaspoons heavy cream
1½ teaspoons bottled demiglace
Seasoned salt and pepper

Fresh lemon
1 teaspoon butter

Put all ingredients except lemon and butter in a heavy skillet and reduce mixture over medium heat to half its original volume. Just before serving, swirl in a squeeze of fresh lemon and the teaspoon of butter.

Fig Sauce for Roast Duckling

Fine with pheasant as well.

4 fresh or dried figs
4 tablespoons port
1 level teaspoon ground cinnamon
1 teaspoon sugar
4 tablespoons unsalted butter
Pinch of salt
2 tablespoons red wine vinegar
1 tablespoon minced shallots
½ cup demiglace
Seasoned salt
Freshly ground black pepper

Place the figs, port, cinnamon, sugar, 1 tablespoon butter and a pinch of salt in a small skillet. Cover and simmer gently for 15–20 minutes, or until figs are tender and have absorbed most of the liquid. Purée the figs in a food processor with 2 tablespoons of butter.

In a saucepan, put the vinegar, shallots, 1 tablespoon butter and demiglace. Let the sauce simmer and reduce for 1–2 minutes. Turn off heat and add the fig mixture. Season with salt and pepper, pass the sauce through a sieve into a small saucepan and reheat for about 1 minute. Serve immediately over crispy roast duckling. Makes about 1 cup.

Mustard Sauce

Excellent served on the side with gravlax or grilled fish.

¼ cup creole mustard
¼ cup Dijon mustard
6 tablespoons white vinegar
6 tablespoons sugar
Seasoned salt to taste
Freshly ground pepper to taste
1 cup oil
1 cup chopped fresh dill
2 tablespoons cognac

Put the two mustards, the vinegar, sugar, salt and pepper in a mixing bowl. Start beating with a wire whisk while adding the oil in a slow, thin, steady stream. When all the oil is added, stir in the dill and cognac. Another pinch of pepper may be needed.

Pasta

Garlic's taste is briefest pleasure—
Eat in haste, repent in leisure.
Garlic's like the poor, like sorrow—
Here today and here tomorrow.
JUSTIN RICHARDSON

COMES NOW THE SECTION of this book wherein Tony Vallone speaks with the utmost personal authority, where his Italian-ness manifests itself with confidence and gusto: Pasta. Tony might have heard the old saying of an unknown culinary pundit who said that "Garlic is the catsup of intellectuals," but Tony might perhaps wish to rephrase it: "Garlic is the catsup of my pasta recipes." He uses it in abundance and with marvelous results.

It has been said that pasta is a paste made of flour, water, salt and Italian inspiration. Most of these inspired pasta dishes may be served either as an appetizer or as a main course, as they are at the restaurant; just plan your quantities accordingly. The recipes usually call for one pound of pasta, which will serve anywhere from three to ten people, depending upon whether the dish is served as appetizer or main course. "The rule of thumb," says Tony, "is three to four ounces of pasta per person, as a main course."

Pasta with Anchovies

1 pound fidelini or spaghettini
8 tablespoons extra virgin olive oil
4 cloves garlic, minced
10–12 anchovy fillets, rinsed and chopped
Freshly ground black pepper
Pinch of crushed red pepper
8 basil leaves, torn into pieces
Fresh chopped parsley

Heat the oil and sauté the garlic over medium heat until opaque. Add the anchovies and cook until soft. Add both peppers, the basil and a good bit of chopped parsley. Simmer 1 minute more. Serve over *al dente* pasta that has a little water left in it (do not drain completely). Mix pasta and sauce well with a little more parsley sprinkled on top and serve immediately.

WINE: *In Richard Dewey's words, "A big, booming Gavi" or Sancerre*

Pasta with Vodka

A rich, creamy, thoroughly wonderful dish. Grappa makes a zippy alternative to the vodka.

1 pound fidelini or linguine
7 tablespoons unsalted butter
1/2–3/4 teaspoon red pepper flakes
3/4 cup vodka (Russian or Polish)
1 cup canned Italian tomatoes, drained and puréed
3/4 cup heavy cream
1 teaspoon seasoned salt
1 cup Parmesan cheese, freshly grated
8 leaves fresh sweet basil, shredded

Warm the bowl in which you intend to serve the pasta. Melt the butter in a large skillet; add the pepper flakes and vodka and simmer for 2 minutes. Add the tomatoes and cream and simmer for 5 minutes. Add the salt and stir well.

As soon as the pasta is *al dente*, drain well and add to the skillet with the hot sauce. With the flame on low, add the Parmesan and mix thoroughly. Pour into the heated bowl, top with the fresh sweet basil, toss well and serve immediately. Serves 6.

WINE: *Vino Nobile di Montepulciano*

Aunt Mary's Baked Macaroni with Three Cheeses

1 pound penne or macaroni of choice
3 tablespoons butter
1 cup freshly grated Parmesan cheese
½ cup ricotta cheese
½ cup grated mozzarella cheese
1½ cups heavy cream
Pinch of nutmeg
Pinch of seasoned salt
Good pinch of freshly ground white pepper
Pinch of cayenne pepper

Use any shape of cut pasta you prefer. Cook until *al dente*. Drain, rinse under cold water and drain again.

In a buttered casserole, toss the macaroni with the butter, then the 3 cheeses and mix well. Meanwhile, combine the cream, nutmeg, salt and peppers. Pour the cream mixture over the pasta, mix well and bake in a preheated 400° oven for about 20 minutes, or until browned. Serves 6–8.

WINE: *Picolit or Riesling or Frascati*

Thieves' Pasta

Tony: "I like this dish spicy and add a little more crushed red pepper over each portion. There are many variations to this southern Italian dish. In Corleone my cousin added fresh fennel and chopped raisins and it was fabulous."

1 pound penne, fusilli, ziti or other cut pasta
½ cup Italian extra virgin olive oil
4 large garlic cloves, minced
4–5 cups very ripe tomatoes, peeled, seeded and chopped or *36 ounces Italian canned tomatoes, juice and all*
4–6 tablespoons dry white wine
1 tablespoon sugar
Seasoned salt and freshly ground white pepper
3 cups broccoli florets, precooked firm
1½–2 cups fresh spinach washed, drained, chopped
½ cup pine nuts (slightly prebrowned in oven)
Crushed red pepper flakes
4–6 ounces Mascarpone cheese, at room temperature

Combine olive oil and garlic in a large heavy saucepan over low heat and sauté until the garlic begins to turn opaque. Add tomatoes (if canned, break them up with a wooden spoon as you stir), wine, sugar, salt and a generous sprinkling of white pepper. Increase heat to medium and continue cooking, stirring frequently for 12–15 minutes. Add broccoli, spinach, pine nuts, a dash of crushed red pepper flakes and cook stirring for 5–7 minutes. Add the Mascarpone little by little, stirring all the while. (Sauce should be slightly pink in color.) Pour just cooked and drained *al dente* penne into the sauce and toss well. Serve immediately. Serves 8–10 as an appetizer and 6–8 as an entree.

Note: Cream cheese may be substituted for the Mascarpone, but it will not be as good.

WINE: *A big Burgundy or Chianti*

Pasta Pizzaiola

1 pound fidelini or capellini
2 peppers (1 red and 1 yellow, or 2 of either)
4 tablespoons extra virgin olive oil
6 cloves garlic, minced
1 28-ounce can Italian tomatoes (juice and all)
1 scant tablespoon capers, rinsed and drained
8 black olives, sliced lengthwise
Pinch of sugar
Seasoned salt and freshly ground black pepper
Pinch of crushed red pepper
Pinch of dried oregano
2–3 fresh basil leaves (torn in 3 pieces each)
2 tablespoons red wine

Core, seed, and slice the peppers into julienne strips. In a large heavy skillet, heat the olive oil and add the garlic. As the garlic begins to turn an opaque color, add the peppers. Sauté the peppers for a minute or so, stirring (do not let the garlic burn). Break up the tomatoes and add them to the skillet. Sauté, stirring with a wooden spoon until the tomatoes begin to thicken a little. Add capers, olives, sugar, salt, black pepper and crushed red pepper. Do not be stingy with the peppers as this should be a spicy sauce. Simmer for 5 minutes, stirring occasionally. Add oregano, basil and wine and simmer 5 more minutes, stirring. Serve over *al dente* fidelini or capellini. This sauce is also excellent with shellfish added to it.

WINE: *Chianti*

Spaghetti alla Turiddu

A Sicilian classic, and pungent with garlic.

PASTA

1 pound spaghetti, linguine or capellini
½ cup light olive oil
4 cloves garlic, crushed in a garlic press
6 anchovy fillets, rinsed and pounded to a paste
2 teaspoons capers
½ cup Gaeta or other Sicilian-style olives, rinsed, pitted and chopped
1 28-ounce can Italian tomatoes, or *1½ pounds fresh tomatoes, drained and chopped*
1 tablespoon red wine
½ teaspoon seasoned salt
½ teaspoon ground white pepper
1 tablespoon chopped fresh basil
1 teaspoon dried oregano
1 tablespoon chopped fresh parsley

Put the olive oil and the garlic in a heavy saucepan and sauté over medium heat until the garlic turns a light gold. Add the anchovies, capers, olives, tomatoes, wine, salt and pepper and bring to a light boil. Lower heat and simmer for 12–15 minutes, then add the basil, oregano and parsley. Cook 1 more minute and serve, mixed well, over *al dente* pasta. Serves 4–6.

WINE: *Regaleali (a red Sicilian wine) or a California Zinfandel (red)*

Spaghetti al Magro, Siciliano

When Tony was a child, this meatless dish was Friday's dinner.

1–1½ pounds spaghetti
1 small eggplant
Salt
½ cup Italian olive oil
1 large clove garlic, minced
½ small onion, minced
6 cups Spicy Marinara Sauce (see page 86)
¼ cup minced parsley
3 tablespoons fresh basil, minced, or *1½ teaspoons dried*
2 tablespoons capers
15 pitted black olives, minced
4 anchovy fillets, minced
¼ teaspoon crushed red pepper

Wash eggplant and cut into ½-inch cubes. Put into a bowl, sprinkle with salt and let stand for 1 hour. Drain (this removes the moisture from the eggplant).

Heat the oil in a heavy saucepan. Add garlic and onion. Cook, stirring constantly, until onion is soft. Add marinara and simmer, covered, for 6–8 minutes. Add all remaining ingredients. Check salt, adding only if necessary. Usually, it will not be needed. Simmer, covered, over low heat for about 25 minutes. Serves 6–8.

WINE: *A dry Sicilian white, such as Greco di Tufo, or Corvo Bianco*

Spaghettini with Tomatoes and Mushrooms

1 pound imported spaghettini, linguine or fidelini
5 tablespoons extra virgin olive oil
4–5 cloves garlic, minced
2 cups very ripe tomatoes, peeled, seeded and chopped
¼ cup very dry white wine
1 teaspoon sugar
Seasoned salt and freshly ground white pepper
¾ pound mixed fresh mushrooms in any combination (shiitake, porcini, oyster, cèpes, enoki, chanterelles, etc.)
8–10 leaves fresh basil, torn into pieces
Crushed red pepper flakes

Heat olive oil in a large heavy skillet over medium heat. Stir in garlic and sauté a minute or two until garlic begins to become opaque. Next add tomatoes and wine and sauté, stirring for 3–5 minutes. Add sugar, seasoned salt and a generous dash of white pepper. Cook, stirring, another minute or so and add the mushrooms and basil and a good pinch of crushed red pepper. Cook, stirring another minute or so and spoon immediately over *al dente* pasta. Serve with freshly grated Parmesan cheese to the side. (Mushrooms should still be firm; do not overcook.) Serves 4–6.

WINE: *Sancerre or Barolo*

Spaghetti 'In Fretta'

Pasta done in a hurry, quick and easy.

1 pound imported spaghetti
3 tablespoons of the spaghetti water
1 tablespoon Italian extra virgin olive oil
1 cup freshly grated Romano or Parmesan cheese

Handful (loosely packed) fresh basil shredded into medium pieces
1–1½ teaspoons freshly grated white pepper

Cook the spaghetti in plenty of rapidly boiling salted water and drain at the *al dente* stage. Put into a hot serving casserole or bowl and pour over the spaghetti water and olive oil and toss. Next, scatter the cheese, basil and pepper and mix well. (You may want a little more olive oil.) Serve immediately. Serves 4–6.

WINE: *Chianti*

Fettuccine Alfredo

A Roman classic. The better the quality of pasta and Parmesan, the better the dish.

1 pound fresh fettuccine or imported dry fettuccine
5 tablespoons unsalted butter
1–1½ cups heavy cream
¾ cup freshly grated Romano or Parmesan cheese
Freshly ground black pepper

Cook fettuccine in 3 quarts salted boiling water with a few drops of olive oil in it for 1½ minutes if fresh, about 6 minutes if dried. Drain well.

Meanwhile, melt butter in a large saucepan or frying pan. Add fettuccine to the pan and toss well. Stir in the cream and cook for 2 minutes, tossing well. Add about ⅓ or a little more (to taste) of the freshly grated cheese and mix well. Serve immediately with the remaining cheese and freshly grated black pepper.

WINE: *Orvieto (dry) or Frascati*

Fettuccine Carbonara

When done correctly, this is one of the great pasta dishes. The trick lies in having a very hot bowl and a hot pancetta mixture and in vigorously tossing the hot pasta with the room-temperature egg-cream mixture.

1 pound fettuccine
1/3 cup pancetta (Italian bacon) cut into 1/2-inch pieces
Crushed red pepper flakes
Freshly ground black pepper
2 whole eggs, plus 2 yolks, at room temperature
1 cup heavy cream, at room temperature
1 cup Parmesan cheese, freshly grated
4 tablespoons butter, softened
Seasoned salt
1/2–2/3 cup peas (optional)

In a heavy sauté skillet, cook the pancetta slowly until done. The pancetta should be slightly crisp. Stir in a pinch of crushed red pepper flakes and a good dash of black pepper. Remove pan from heat, but keep hot.

Beat the eggs and egg yolks together so they are well mixed. Add the cream and 1/2 cup of the Parmesan and beat again to mix well.

When the pasta is cooked *al dente*, have a warmed large flameproof mixing bowl and a casserole ready (warm the bowl by rinsing it in very hot water and put it in the oven). Quickly put the drained pasta into the bowl and add the softened butter and mix the fettuccine well so that all strands are coated with the butter. Meanwhile, reheat the pancetta mixture and pour hot over the buttered pasta and mix well. Put the mixing bowl over a low heat and pour the egg-cream mixture over the pasta, tossing constantly with two large forks. At this point, you might need to add a pinch of salt. The bowl and pasta should have been hot enough to cook the egg mixture and the pasta must be tossed well and served immediately. A variation is to toss in slightly cooked, still hot and firm peas immediately after adding the egg-cream mixture. Offer freshly grated Parmesan with the pasta.

WINE: *Orvieto (dry, not the sweet)*

Capellini Frittata

(From Van Jones and Jack Mastroianni)

Combine the following in a large bowl:

1 pound capellini, cooked al dente, *lightly buttered*
1 pound pancetta or bacon, chopped, fried until crisp and drained
4 eggs, beaten
A generous amount of Parmesan cheese
Salt and pepper to taste
Red pepper (optional)

In an oval or round skillet, melt 1 tablespoon butter and when the foam subsides, add the pasta mixture (which should be at room temperature). Spread it evenly and cook over medium heat for about 10 minutes, shaking the pan occasionally to keep it from sticking and moving the pan once or twice to brown the bottom evenly. When it begins to smell "done," turn it out into a plate, add more butter to the pan and repeat for the other side. Cut up and serve lukewarm.

WINE: *Pinot Grigio or a white Chianti*

Capellini Frittata with Pancetta and Peas

This can easily be prepared in advance and warmed later or served at room temperature.

PASTA

4 eggs, lightly beaten
1 cup capellini, broken into 2-inch pieces and cooked al dente
1 cup freshly grated mozzarella cheese
Seasoned salt and freshly ground black pepper
Pinch red pepper flakes
6 very thick slices of pancetta (Italian bacon), cut into small pieces and cooked crisp
1 cup fresh or frozen peas, lightly cooked
1/3 cup freshly grated Parmesan cheese
3 tablespoons Italian olive oil
3 cloves garlic, pressed in a garlic press

In a medium bowl, combine the eggs, cooked capellini, mozzarella, salt and peppers (season to taste). Mix very well and set aside. In another small bowl, mix the pancetta, peas and Parmesan cheese. Combine gently but thoroughly.

In a large non-stick skillet, heat the oil, add the garlic and sauté over medium-high heat for 1 minute. Pour ½ the egg and pasta mixture into the skillet and top with all the pancetta, peas and cheese. Cover with the remaining half of the egg and pasta mixture. Cook for 8–9 minutes, pressing the mixture down slightly.

Invert the frittata onto a large plate and slide it back into the pan. You might need to add a little more olive oil to the pan for this step. Cook the underside for 5 minutes or less, or until golden brown. Serve warm or allow to cool for later.

WINE: *Cannellino, a sweet Frascati*

Capellini with Sun-dried Tomato Pesto

1 pound capellini
1 cup olive oil from sun-dried tomatoes (or add extra virgin olive oil to equal 1 cup)
1 cup sun-dried tomatoes, cut into thin strips
8 large fresh sweet basil leaves
1 teaspoon crushed red pepper

Combine ¼ cup olive oil and ½ cup of the sun-dried tomatoes, the basil and the red pepper in a food processor. Process until the tomatoes become a rough paste. In a bowl, combine this paste with the remaining oil. Cook the capellini *al dente* (careful not to overcook); drain. Gently toss the capellini in a large bowl with the olive oil and tomato paste mixture. Scatter the remaining tomato strips over the pasta and serve immediately.

WINE: *Amarone*

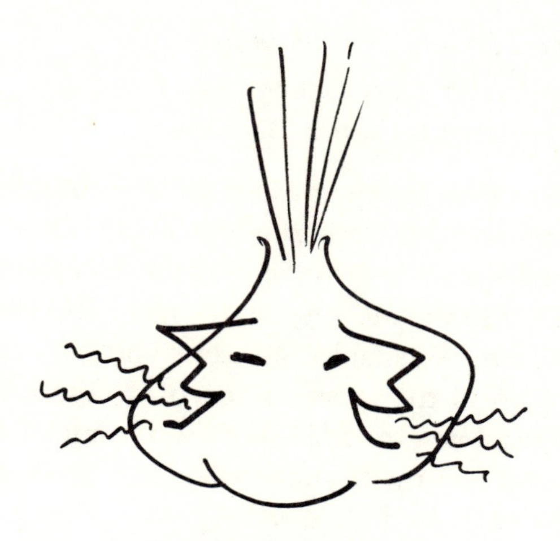

. . . Here today and here tomorrow.

Linguine con Verdure

Tony: "This pasta-with-vegetable recipe is often an icebox-cleaning dish at our house. It has endless variations."

1½ pounds linguine
1 small bunch broccoli, cut into florets, leaving a short stem
10 florets cauliflower
12–16 asparagus tips
½ cup sliced black olives
1 cup fresh or frozen peas
12 tablespoons butter, divided
8–12 pieces dried porcini mushrooms, washed and presoaked in dry sherry and chopped
Pinch of nutmeg
4 fresh sweet basil leaves, chopped
¾ cup heavy cream
Salt and freshly ground white pepper
¾ cup freshly grated Parmesan cheese
¾ cup marinara sauce (optional)

Cook vegetables in salted boiling water for 3–5 minutes (cook peas 1½ minutes, no more). Drain and run under cold water. When cool, cut larger vegetables into ½-inch pieces. In a saucepan, melt 8½ tablespoons butter; add the mushrooms, nutmeg and basil and cook for 5 minutes. Add the vegetables and cook another 5 minutes, stirring occasionally. Add the cream, a pinch of salt and a generous dash of pepper and bring to a simmer for 3 minutes. Melt the remaining butter and toss the freshly cooked and drained linguine in the butter until well coated. Add the vegetable cream mixture and toss well. Add ½ the cheese and toss again. Serve immediately with a dash of pepper on top and grated Parmesan to the side. For a tasty and colorful variation, spoon a dollop of hot marinara sauce on the top. Serves 6–8.

WINE: *Frascati*

Linguine Bucaniera

1 pound imported linguine
½ cup light extra virgin olive oil
4 cloves garlic, crushed in a garlic press
1 28-ounce can imported Italian tomatoes
1 tablespoon red wine or dry Marsala
½–1 teaspoon freshly ground white pepper
1 level teaspoon seasoned salt
Meat from 1 small lobster and medium lobster tail, cut into pieces
¼ pound squid, cleaned and diced
1 pound clams, steamed, shelled and chopped
Pinch dried red pepper flakes
3 tablespoons chopped parsley

Put ½ the oil into a large, heavy saucepan over medium heat and almost brown the garlic in it. Add the tomatoes, wine, pepper and salt and continue cooking over low heat 12–15 minutes. Heat the rest of the oil in another saucepan. Add the lobster meat and squid and cook for 4–6 minutes. Add the clams, cook for a minute more and remove from the heat. Combine all the seafood with the tomato sauce. Heat through. Pour onto freshly cooked and drained *al dente* linguine. Mix and serve at once with chopped parsley on top as garnish.

WINE: *Soave*

Linguine alle Vongole

1 pound imported linguine
5 dozen fresh small clams
3 tablespoons Italian olive oil
1 tablespoon chopped garlic
½ tablespoon chopped fresh parsley
Freshly ground black pepper
Pinch of oregano
Pinch crushed red pepper
Clam juice (optional)

Wash clams thoroughly under cold water and open over mixing bowl so as not to lose any clam juice (clams may also be steamed lightly to open). Remove clams carefully and discard shells. Save a whole opened clam per serving as a garnish later. Chop the clams into small pieces, saving all the juices.

Heat olive oil in a saucepan and sauté garlic until golden. Add some clam juice, parsley, black pepper, oregano and crushed red pepper. Then, add clams and cook about 3 minutes. Remove from heat, add more clam juice if desired (generally, a little more is needed), and cook 2 minutes more. Serve immediately over linguine.

WINE: *Gavi or Pinot Grigio*

Linguine and Cream Clam Sauce

1 pound imported or fresh linguine
24 cherrystone clams or *1 cup canned clams plus 1½ cups clam juice*
4 cups water
Seasoned salt to taste
1 cup heavy cream
8 tablespoons unsalted butter
1½ tablespoons finely chopped garlic
4 tablespoons finely chopped parsley
3 tablespoons finely chopped basil
½ teaspoon dried thyme
Pinch crushed red pepper
Freshly ground pepper to taste
½ cup grated Parmesan cheese

Open and drain the clams and reserve both clams and juice. Chop the clams. Pour the juice into a kettle and add the water and salt. Bring to a boil and cook linguine *al dente*. Meanwhile, for the sauce:

Heat the cream in a saucepan just to a boil. Heat half the butter in another saucepan and add the clams, garlic, herbs and peppers. Mix well and add the cream. Mix well. When the linguine is done, drain it quickly and place in a large warmed platter or bowl. Add the sauce immediately (this must be done quickly so the pasta won't stick). Add the remaining butter and the cheese and a pinch of salt. Toss well and serve immediately. Serves 4–6.

WINE: *Gavi or Pinot Grigio or Soave*

Linguine Salsa Cruda

This simple sauce is excellent not only on pasta but also on grilled fish or veal.

1 pound imported linguine
4 pounds firm, ripe, very red tomatoes
4–6 cloves garlic, minced
3/4 cup chopped fresh basil leaves
1 cup Italian extra virgin olive oil
Seasoned salt and freshly ground pepper

Plunge the tomatoes into boiling water for 5 seconds. Peel, cool, seed and dice the tomatoes. Combine with the garlic, basil and olive oil in a bowl. Season to taste with the salt and pepper. Marinate at room temperature for 1 hour. Makes about 6 cups.

Cook the linguine *al dente*. Quickly toss the hot pasta with the *salsa cruda* and serve immediately. Serves 6–8.

WINE: *A Cabernet from the Grave del Friuli zone or Chianti*

Linguine with Porcini and Eggplant

1 pound imported linguine
1/2 cup porcini (Italian dried mushrooms), well rinsed
1 medium eggplant, diced, but not too small (1 1/2-2 inches)
1/2 cup good Italian olive oil

2 cloves garlic, chopped fine
2½ cups chopped canned Italian tomatoes with some liquid
2 tablespoons red wine
½ teaspoon red pepper flakes
Pinch of sugar
2 tablespoons chopped fresh parsley
1 tablespoon chopped fresh basil
Seasoned salt
Freshly ground black pepper
2 tablespoons butter, softened
6 tablespoons freshly grated Romano cheese
¾ cup fresh ricotta (optional)

Put the porcini in a small bowl and cover with warm water; let stand for about 30 minutes. Meanwhile, spread diced eggplant out on paper towels. Sprinkle with salt and let drain for 30 minutes.

In a large skillet, heat the olive oil over medium-high heat and sauté the eggplant cubes on all sides for about 12–15 minutes. Stir them frequently and do not be alarmed at how much oil they absorb. Add the garlic and sauté, stirring for 2 minutes. Add the tomatoes, wine, red peppers, sugar, parsley, basil, salt and pepper. Drain the mushrooms well and add them to the skillet. Bring this mixture to a light boil, lower the heat and simmer 25–30 minutes, or until eggplant cubes are tender. Correct seasonings if needed.

When the sauce is about two-thirds done, cook the linguine *al dente*. Drain it well and return to the empty pot it was cooked in, tossing well with the softened butter. Add the sauce and toss very well. Serve in individual bowls, topped with freshly grated Romano or Parmesan cheese. For an extra touch, add a small dollop (a teaspoon or less) of fresh ricotta in the center of each serving. Serves 6–8.

WINE: *Chianti*

Fidelini alla Arrabbiata

Arrabbiata means angry. This dish derives its name from its spicy-hot flavor.

PASTA

1 pound imported fidelini, capellini or linguine
1 pound Italian sweet sausage, removed from casing
¼ cup Italian extra virgin olive oil
2 tablespoons minced garlic
28 to 56 ounces canned imported Italian tomatoes, juice and all
¼ cup red wine
Seasoned salt and a generous amount of fresh black pepper
½ teaspoon crushed red pepper or more if desired
1 teaspoon sugar
1 tablespoon capers
1 tablespoon fresh parsley, chopped
4 fresh basil leaves torn into pieces
Generous pinch dried oregano (optional)
1 10-ounce package frozen artichokes, cooked and drained

Heat oil in a heavy saucepan and cook garlic until almost golden. Add sausage meat in small chunks; brown. Add the tomatoes, wine, salt, both peppers and sugar. Cook over a medium heat for about 15 minutes, stirring and breaking up the tomatoes with a wooden spoon. Add the capers, parsley, basil, oregano and artichokes and simmer 5 more minutes. Serve over *al dente* pasta, with freshly grated Parmesan cheese to the side, if desired.

WINE: *Fiano di Avellino or Sancerre or Barolo.*

Fidelini Sicilian Style

1 pound fidelini or linguine
1 cup extra virgin olive oil
2 cloves garlic, minced
1 28-ounce can Italian tomatoes
1 tablespoon chopped fresh parsley
Pinch crushed red pepper (about 1/4 teaspoon)
Seasoned salt and freshly ground black pepper
1 tablespoon capers, rinsed
6 anchovy fillets or *4 sardines, minced*
4 ounces tuna
1–2 ounces slivered almonds, prebrowned in oven
Pinch of dried oregano (about 1/2 teaspoon)

Heat the olive oil in a large, heavy skillet. Add the garlic. As it begins to turn opaque, add the tomatoes, stirring and breaking them with a wooden spoon. Cook for 3–5 minutes and add parsley, both peppers and seasoned salt. Next, add capers, anchovies or sardines and tuna. Let simmer for 5–7 minutes and add the almonds and oregano. Serve immediately over *al dente* pasta.

WINE: *Sangiovese or Corvo*

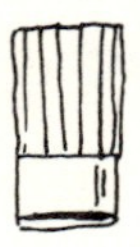

Baked Ziti with Sausage and Ricotta

Try this in place of your old recipe for lasagna. It is a crowd-pleaser that can be prepared in advance.

1 pound ziti or other macaroni
1 pound Italian sausage
1 pound ricotta
1 egg
¼ cup minced fresh parsley
6 cups Spicy Marinara Sauce (page 86)
1 pound mozzarella, grated
1½ cups freshly grated Romano or Parmesan

Prick the sausage with a fork several times, and put in a baking pan in the oven at 400° for 30 minutes. Prepare the marinara. When sausage is done, discard the fat, transfer the sausage to a cutting board and let cool for 15 minutes; cut it into ¼-inch slices.

Cook the ziti *al dente*. Meanwhile, combine the ricotta, egg and parsley in a bowl and mix well. Drain the ziti thoroughly.

Coat the bottom of a 15×10×2½-inch baking pan with 2 cups of the tomato sauce. On the sauce, layer half the ziti, half the ricotta mixture, half the sausage, half the mozzarella and half the Parmesan or Romano and cover the mixture with 2 more cups of marinara. Layer the remaining ziti, ricotta, sausage and mozzarella. Cover the mixture with the remaining sauce, and sprinkle it with the remaining ¾ cup Romano or Parmesan. Bake in a 375° oven for 45 minutes to 1 hour, or until bubbling. Remove from oven, let it rest for 3–5 minutes before serving. Serves 6–8 as a main course.

WINE: *Barbera d'Asti or Gattinara*

Seafood

Fish must swim thrice—once in water,
a second time in the sauce and [a] third time
in wine in the stomach.

JOHN RAY

EACH OF US KNOWS MORE than one kind of hunger, including the wistful hunger created by memories of glorious meals in our past, and the hunger born of expectation. The last is the hunger of someone who may not be hungry but who anticipates dining at home or at a restaurant, knowing that something longed for may be expected—a favorite tuna fish salad at home, say, or Quenelles of Trout with Saffron Sauce at the restaurant. The first is the hunger illumined by Julian Street: "When we let our thoughts turn back to the most interesting episodes of our life, there is almost always a memory of a meal or a bottle somewhere in the picture—a kindly ghost of food or drink enjoyed long ago, now to be savored only in the mind, which is, after all, the place where remembered meals and bottles are finally digested."

It is hard to single out one thing more than another at Tony's, but many know "the hunger of someone who may not be hungry" when thinking of the restaurant's seafood dishes, and of the beguiling seafood with pasta. It is said that restaurants are more skillful in preparing seafood than is possible at home, but that depends on the cook—either place. All that can be said is that as a rule a professional kitchen has more tools, more equipment, than a home. In any case, Tony's two overriding rules of seafood cookery are: the seafood must be as fresh as possible; and it must *never* be overcooked. With these two caveats in mind, the cook will find that the following recipes work well at home.

Simple Whole Grilled Fish

1 red snapper, redfish, trout or comparable fish, about 2½ pounds, cleaned but left whole, with head and tail on (at least the tail!)
4 large cloves garlic
4 fresh mint leaves
2 tablespoons fresh rosemary
Seasoned salt and freshly ground black pepper
1 bay leaf
5–6 tablespoons Italian extra virgin olive oil
Lemon halves

Preheat the oven to 450°. Cut each clove of garlic into 4 pieces. Make 2 slits on each side of the fish and insert a mint leaf, some rosemary and 3 pieces of garlic in each slit. Season the cavity of the fish with the seasoned salt and pepper. Place the bay leaf in the cavity with the remaining garlic and rosemary, and dribble 1 tablespoon of the olive oil over this. With your fingertips, rub the outside of the fish with olive oil and then season the outside of the fish with seasoned salt and pepper.

Put fish directly on middle shelf of the oven (about 4–6 inches from broiler) and broil for about 12–14 minutes on each side. (Make sure you have a pan underneath the fish to catch the drippings.)

Sprinkle a little olive oil and squeeze fresh lemon on each serving. Serves 4.

WINE: *Frascati*

Red Snapper Noisette

A delicious entree served at Tony's for many years.

4 fillets of fresh red snapper
1 cup flour, seasoned with salt and pepper to taste
9–10 tablespoons butter
6 large mushrooms, sliced into T-shapes
1 pound fresh lump crabmeat
4 lemons cut into halves
Parsley

Dredge red snapper fillets in seasoned flour. Sauté them in skillet in 4–5 tablespoons of the butter until crispy on both sides. Remove and keep warm in oven.

In another skillet, cook the rest of the butter over medium heat until it is golden brown. Add the mushrooms to the butter only after it is nice and dark. Remove them from the hot butter after 30 seconds. Arrange the red snapper on plates with crabmeat on top and spoon mushrooms and *beurre noisette* over. Squeeze ½ lemon over each and serve immediately with parsley garnish and additional lemon. Serves 4.

WINE: *California Chardonnay or Meursault*

Stuffed Red Snapper

1 5- to 6-pound red snapper, redfish or trout
2½ teaspoons seasoned salt
1 teaspoon black pepper
3 cloves garlic, minced
4 tablespoons Italian olive oil
2 cups fresh bread crumbs
½ cup chopped yellow onion
½ cup chopped celery
½ cup chopped parsley
¼ teaspoon crushed red pepper flakes
Pinch of dried oregano
2 tablespoons unsalted butter
¾ cup dry white wine
2 lemon halves

Have the fish split and boned for stuffing. Leave the head and/or tail on if desired. Wash and dry the fish and rub inside and out with salt, black pepper, garlic and olive oil.

Soak the bread crumbs in water and drain. Sauté the onion and celery in the olive oil for about 8–10 minutes. Add the parsley, red pepper flakes, oregano and soaked bread crumbs, mixing thoroughly. Stuff the fish with this mixture and sew the fish or fasten with skewers. Melt the butter in a large baking pan. Place the fish in it. Pour wine over all and bake in a preheated 400° oven for about 40–45 minutes, or until done (do not overcook). Transfer to a warmed serving platter, squeeze lemon juice over and serve immediately. Serves 4–6.

WINE: *Vouvray*

Aunt Mary's Red Snapper

2 1½–pound red snappers, cleaned
½ cup unsalted butter, divided
Seasoned salt and freshly ground black pepper
½ cup dry vermouth or white wine
Bouquet garni: 2 sprigs thyme (or ¼ teaspoon dried), 1 bay leaf, 2 sprigs parsley
½ cup fish stock or bouillon
1 medium onion, chopped
1½ pounds pear tomatoes, puréed in blender or processor, or chopped fine
Cayenne

Melt 4 tablespoons of butter over a fairly high heat in a large pan. When the butter begins to brown, add the fish and brown quickly on both sides. Season with salt and pepper, add the wine, bouquet garni, and fish stock or bouillon. Cover the pan and bring to a boil. Reduce heat and simmer 8–10 minutes.

While the fish are cooking, melt the remaining butter in a saucepan over medium heat. Add the onion and cook until golden. Add the tomatoes, season with salt and pepper, and cook over high heat for about 15 minutes.

When the fish are cooked, transfer them to a hot serving dish and keep warm. Discard the bouquet garni, reduce the fish cooking liquid to about 3 tablespoons, add it to the tomatoes, add a pinch of cayenne and cook 2 minutes more. Pour sauce over fish and serve immediately. Serves 4.

WINE: *Chardonnay*

Red Snapper Mariniere

4 fillets of red snapper (8–10 ounces each)

For the court bouillon:

½–¾ bottle of dry white wine
2 carrots, sliced
1 onion, sliced
2 tablespoons chopped shallots
4 cloves garlic, peeled
1 lemon, peeled and sliced
Seasoned salt and freshly ground black pepper to taste
Chopped fresh parsley

For the sauce:

6½ tablespoons Italian olive oil
1 tablespoon minced shallots
1 large tomato, peeled, skinned and seeded
Pinch of thyme
1 bay leaf
2 tablespoons lemon juice
4 tablespoons dry white wine
½ cup cold sweet butter
3 tablespoons each, tarragon and fresh basil, chopped

Place all the ingredients for the court bouillon in a large saucepan. Simmer for 30 minutes. Strain and set aside.

Heat the olive oil in a saucepan and add the shallots. Cook shallots until soft. Add the tomato and 1 cup of the court bouillon; the sauce should not be too liquid at this time. Add more salt and especially pepper as needed. Add the thyme, bay leaf and a little lemon juice. Boil for about 7–8 minutes to reduce. While the sauce is reducing, place 4 tablespoons of the wine and the remaining lemon juice in another saucepan and bring to a boil. Whisk in the cold butter, little by little, to form an emulsion, then remove from heat.

Pour the melted butter into the reduced sauce, stirring slowly and constantly. Add the freshly chopped herbs. A pinch or so more pepper may be added at this time. Keep the sauce warm, whisking it now and then.

Heat oven to 550°. Salt and pepper the fish fillets. Place them on a buttered baking dish and bake in hot oven about 10–12 minutes. Place them on plates. Spoon the sauce over and garnish with chopped fresh parsley. Serves 4.

WINE: *A Sicilian white, perhaps Corvo*

Red Snapper with Shrimp and Lump Crab

This dish is the creation of Tony's chef Robert Vasquez.

4 red snapper fillets (6–8 ounces each)
Seasoned salt and freshly ground white pepper
Flour
3/4 cup half-and-half
1 egg, beaten
1 1/2 cups oil
12 ounces lump crabmeat
16 large shrimp (16–18 count), cooked
Beurre blanc (page 128)
2 tablespoons chopped fresh parsley

Season fillets with the salt and a good pinch of the white pepper. Dredge fillets in flour, shaking off any excess. Dip them in a batter made of the half-and-half and egg mixed well. Fry fillets in the oil in a large skillet until brown and crispy on both sides. Remove and drain well on paper towels.

Top each fillet with lump crabmeat and shrimp arranged alternately. (Shrimp may be cut in half lengthwise, if desired. It's also a good idea to prewarm the crab and shrimp in the oven just until hot, but be careful not to allow the crabmeat to dry out.) Pour beurre blanc over each serving (about 1–2 tablespoons sauce per fillet). Sprinkle fresh parsley over all and serve immediately. Serves 4.

BEURRE BLANC:

2 tablespoons minced shallot
1/4 cup fresh lemon juice
1/4 cup dry white wine
1 tablespoon cold water
1/2 cup cold unsalted butter, cut into bits
Freshly ground white pepper and salt

In a small heavy stainless steel or enameled saucepan, cook the shallot with the lemon juice and wine until the liquid is reduced to about 2 tablespoons. Remove pan from heat and add 1 tablespoon cold water. Reduce heat to low and whisk in the butter, 1 piece at a time, lifting pan from heat occasionally to cool mixture and adding each new piece before the previous one has completely melted. Whisk in the white pepper and salt to taste. Makes about 2/3 cup.

WINE: *A dry white Sauvignon or a Gavi*

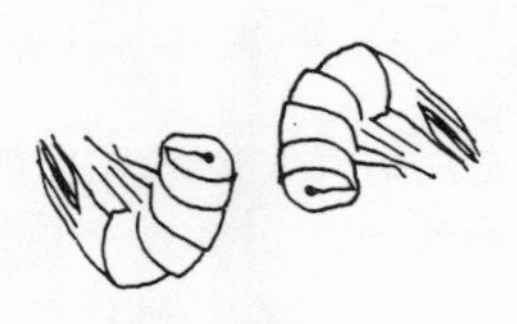

Red Snapper Hemingway

Tony: "Simple and delicious; I like it with the sesame seeds." Try it with the Lime Butter Sauce on page 90.

4 fillets red snapper (6–8 ounces each)
4 tablespoons fresh lemon juice, lemon wedges
3 tablespoons Worcestershire sauce
Seasoned salt and freshly ground black pepper
Flour
1 egg, beaten
1/4 cup milk
1 cup (or more) grated Parmesan cheese
3 tablespoons butter
4 tablespoons Italian olive oil
Sesame seeds, lightly toasted (optional)

Preheat oven to 400°. Combine lemon juice and Worcestershire sauce and sprinkle all over both sides of fish and let fish marinate, turning occasionally, for 15 minutes.

Season fish on both sides with salt and a generous dash of pepper and dredge in flour, shaking off excess. Meanwhile, in a small bowl, combine the egg and milk and beat to mix. Next, dip the fish in the egg-milk mixture and then the grated cheese. Be sure to coat the fish well.

In a heavy skillet, over moderate-high heat, heat the olive oil and butter, and when very hot, add the fish fillets and sauté about 2 minutes on each side, or until browned. Place the skillet in the oven to finish cooking the fish, about 4–5 minutes. *Do not overcook.* Serve immediately with lemon wedges. An excellent variation is to mix a handful or so of sesame seeds with the grated cheese. Serves 4.

WINE: *Corton-Charlemagne*

Roulades of Redfish

Tony: "This was Chef Marc Cox's creation and a wonderful dish."

SEAFOOD

4 2½-ounce pieces of redfish fillet, pounded thin
Flour
3 tablespoons clarified butter

Stuffing:

2 ounces bay scallops
1½ ounces jumbo lump crabmeat
Dash nutmeg
4 ounces Mascarpone cheese
½ teaspoon chopped fresh basil
¼ teaspoon Lea & Perrins sauce
2 drops Tabasco sauce
2 tablespoons heavy cream
1 tablespoon Parmesan cheese
¼ teaspoon chopped parsley
Salt and pepper to taste

Combine all stuffing ingredients. Divide mixture into four parts. Place on pounded redfish fillets. Roll and secure with toothpicks.

Season roulades with salt and pepper. Dredge in flour and sauté over medium heat in clarified butter until lightly browned. Place in 350° oven for 8–10 minutes or until done. Remove toothpicks and arrange roulades on plate. Serve with lemon butter sauce.

Lemon butter sauce:

1 tablespoon lemon juice
2 tablespoons white wine
Dash of Lea & Perrins sauce
Dash each salt and pepper
6 tablespoons butter, softened
1 tablespoon chopped parsley

Place all ingredients except butter in a saucepan. Warm ingredients over medium heat. When warm, whip in soft butter; when smooth add chopped parsley and adjust seasonings. Sauce is ready to spoon over roulades. Serves 2.

WINE: *Fiano di Avellino or Meursault*

Trout Jamaica

One of Tony's personal favorites, a recipe that originated with his friend and mentor, restaurateur Mike Salvato.

4 fillets of fresh trout
Seasoned salt and freshly ground black pepper
1/4 cup oil
1/4 cup butter
1 1/2 cups flour
1 cup milk
4 ounces dark rum
1/2 pound butter
1/2 sweet red pepper, well chopped
2 mushrooms, well chopped
4 lemons, cut in half
1/2-3/4 pound lump crabmeat

Season fillets with salt and pepper and dredge in flour, milk and flour again. Then sauté in oil and butter until crispy on both sides and keep hot in oven. In separate skillet, preheated and very hot, pour the rum and flambé it. Next, add butter, red pepper, mushrooms and juice of 1 lemon. Add crabmeat and let simmer for 3 minutes. Top trout fillets with this mixture, spooning sauce over and adding a squeeze of lemon if needed. Serves 4.

WINE: *California Chardonnay*

Quenelles of Trout with Saffron Sauce

Quenelles are gently poached dumplings, usually flavored with meat or fish.

SEAFOOD

½ pound trout fillet, skinned and well chilled
1 chilled egg white
⅔ cup heavy cream, well chilled
1 tablespoon lemon juice
Seasoned salt and freshly ground black pepper
2⅔ cups fish stock
1 tablespoon butter
4 tablespoons chopped shallots
2 generous pinches saffron threads
½ cup dry white vermouth
½ cup heavy cream
Parsley sprigs

Roughly chop the fish and place in a food processor or blender. Purée until smooth, then slowly add the egg white and cream while the machine is running. When the mixture is firm, stop the machine, add the lemon juice and seasonings, then mix again. Chill until required for cooking.

With two wet spoons, shape the mixture into 12 ovals (quenelles). Poach the quenelles in 2 cups of fish stock for 5–7 minutes, until just firm to the touch. Drain and keep warm.

Meanwhile, to make the sauce, melt the butter and sauté the shallots until soft. Add ⅔ cup fish stock, saffron and white wine, then simmer gently for 5 minutes more. Add the cream and simmer gently again for 5 minutes more. Strain and pour the hot sauce on 4 individual warm plates and arrange 3 quenelles on each. Garnish with parsley. Serves 4.

WINE: *Chablis or a sparkling wine*

Fillets of Trout with Tomatoes and Pesto Sauce

First, make the pesto sauce:

4 ripe tomatoes, peeled and seeded
1 teaspoon minced garlic
1 cup coarsely chopped fresh basil
½ cup olive oil
¼ cup pine nuts, lightly toasted
⅓ cup grated Parmesan cheese
Salt and pepper to taste

Combine ingredients in a blender, processing until fairly smooth.

Now prepare the trout:

6 fillets of trout
4 ripe tomatoes
Butter
Seasoned salt and freshly ground black pepper
½ cup pesto sauce
3 tablespoons butter, cut into bits

Preheat oven to 300°. Peel, slice and seed the tomatoes. Butter a shallow casserole or gratin dish and cover the bottom with half the tomato slices. Season with salt and pepper. Bake 15 minutes. Place the fillets of trout on top of the tomatoes, each fillet folded in half with a tablespoon of heated pesto sauce inside. Cover with the remaining tomato slices. Season again and dot with butter. Broil at high setting 5–10 minutes, or until fish is pure white and flaky. Serve hot or cold, with remaining pesto alongside. Serves 6.

WINE: *Valpolicella or Pinot Grigio*

Trout Parmesan

4 fillets of trout or favorite fish
3/4 cup Italian-style bread crumbs
1/3 cup grated Parmesan cheese
Pinch of paprika
1 teaspoon seasoned salt
Generous sprinkling of freshly ground white pepper
1 teaspoon oregano
1 1/2 tablespoons parsley, chopped fine
Dash of cayenne pepper
1/3 cup flour
2 eggs, beaten
6 tablespoons butter
1 tablespoon oil

Thoroughly mix bread crumbs, cheese, paprika, salt, pepper, oregano, parsley and cayenne.

Dust fillets with flour and dip in beaten eggs, then dip in seasoned bread crumbs, coating thoroughly. Heat butter and oil in a large heavy skillet until very hot but not brown. Fry fish until golden brown and crispy on one side, about 4–5 minutes. Turn carefully and brown the other side (about 3–4 minutes). Drain fish fillets on paper towels and serve immediately with lemon wedges or Spicy Marinara Sauce (page 86). Serves 4.

WINE: *Italian Chardonnay or Frascati*

Fillet of Dover Sole Dugliere

4 18- to 24-ounce fresh dover sole (have your butcher skin and fillet the sole)
Seasoned salt and freshly ground black pepper
3 tablespoons butter
1 small yellow onion, chopped
1½ tablespoons flour
½ cup white wine
¼ cup fish stock
½ cup heavy cream
2 pounds ripe tomatoes, peeled, seeded and chopped
Pinch of cayenne
½ cup fresh sweet basil, torn in pieces
1 teaspoon fresh parsley, chopped
½ cup fresh bread crumbs
Freshly grated Parmesan cheese

Salt and pepper both sides of the sole and place in a well-buttered casserole. Melt 3 tablespoons butter in a saucepan, add the onion and sauté for 2 minutes over a medium-low flame, stirring. Do not brown the onions. Stir in flour. When well mixed and sautéed for a minute, add the wine and fish stock. (If fish stock is not available, add ¼ cup more white wine.) Bring to a boil, stirring, and add the cream, still stirring. Simmer for 5 minutes, season with salt and pepper and add the tomatoes, cayenne, basil and parsley. When well mixed, pour this over the sole. Dust over with bread crumbs and then the cheese. Put in a preheated 400° oven for about 12–15 minutes (do not overcook). Put under the broiler for a minute to brown the top and serve immediately. Serves 4.

WINE: *Puligny-Montrachet or Meursault*

Swordfish Sicilian Style

4 thick-cut swordfish steaks (8–10 ounces each)
3 tablespoons Italian extra virgin olive oil
2 tablespoons finely chopped onion
10 dried black olives, rinsed, pitted and sliced
1 teaspoon minced fresh garlic
Crushed red pepper to taste
2 cups peeled, chopped and drained tomatoes
2 tablespoons red wine
1 teaspoon dried oregano
1 tablespoon finely chopped parsley (the Italian variety, if possible)
1 tablespoon capers
Seasoned salt and freshly ground black pepper
Flour for dredging
Oil for shallow frying

Heat the olive oil in a medium skillet. Add the onion and sauté for 4–5 minutes, stirring. Add olives, garlic and hot pepper flakes and sauté, stirring, for 3 minutes more. Add the tomatoes, wine, oregano, parsley and capers. Cover and simmer 20 minutes.

In the meantime, season the swordfish with salt and pepper on both sides, then dust with flour. Heat about ¾-inch oil in a medium to large skillet. When oil is hot, add fish and quickly brown both sides. Remove from oil and dry with paper towels. Place fish in an ovenproof baking dish and bake in a preheated 500° oven for 5 minutes. (Do not overcook. Swordfish should be served slightly underdone.) Serve immediately with sauce over fish. Rice or angel-hair pasta goes well with this dish. Serves 4.

WINE: *Beaujolais or white Zinfandel or Macon Blanc*

Smothered Shrimp over Rice

Tony's interpretation of a Cajun classic.

1½ pounds raw shrimp, shelled and deveined
¼ cup flour
½ cup butter
1 finely chopped onion
½ cup chopped celery
½ cup chopped green pepper
5–6 cloves garlic, minced
¼ teaspoon crushed red pepper flakes
¼ teaspoon cayenne pepper
½ cup thinly sliced scallions
1 tablespoon lemon juice
½ cup dry white wine
2 tablespoons minced fresh parsley
1 cup water or fish stock
Seasoned salt and freshly ground black pepper

Make a brown roux by combining the flour and butter in a 5-quart saucepan. Cook the roux over medium heat, *stirring constantly*, until it turns golden, about 15–20 minutes.

Add the onion, celery, green pepper and garlic and sauté, stirring, for 15–20 minutes. Add shrimp and remaining ingredients. Bring to a boil, lower heat and simmer 10–12 minutes, or until shrimp are tender, stirring occasionally. Serve over rice. Serves 4–6.

WINE: *California Chardonnay*

Red Peppers with Shrimp Stuffing

Magnificent! Tony calls it "a good home dish."

SEAFOOD

2 large sweet red peppers
3 tablespoons butter
1/4 cup chopped onion
1/4 cup flour
1 cup sour cream at room temperature
Juice of 1 lemon
2 teaspoons Dijon mustard
2 tablespoons chopped fresh parsley
1 8-ounce can water chestnuts, drained and thinly sliced
2 cups very small cooked shrimp
Seasoned salt and freshly ground pepper
1/2 cup shredded Monterey Jack cheese

Preheat oven to 350°. Halve peppers lengthwise and remove seeds and membrane. Blanch for 4 minutes in boiling water, drain and set aside. Melt butter and sauté onion until soft. Sprinkle with flour and cook, stirring until bubbly. Remove from heat and blend in the sour cream. Cook and stir over low heat until thickened. Add lemon juice, mustard, parsley, water chestnuts and shrimp. Season with salt and a good dash of fresh pepper. Spoon into pepper shells and sprinkle tops with cheese. Bake for 30 minutes or until heated through and cheese is bubbly. Serves 4.

WINE: *Muscadet*

Scampi alla Busara

2 pounds very large shrimp, shelled and butterflied, tails left on
1/4 cup Italian olive oil
1 large yellow onion, diced
4–6 large cloves garlic, diced
2 28-ounce cans Italian tomatoes, chopped
1/2 cup dry white wine
1/2 teaspoon dried oregano
Pinch dried thyme
1 tablespoon chopped fresh parsley
1/2 teaspoon seasoned salt
Pinch crushed red pepper flakes
3/4 teaspoon freshly ground black pepper

Heat olive oil in a large saucepan over medium heat. Add onion and sauté about 4 minutes; add garlic and sauté 3 more minutes, stirring occasionally. Add tomatoes and all their juices and cook, stirring occasionally, for about 25 minutes. Much of the liquid will have reduced. Add shrimp and wine to the skillet. Add oregano, thyme, parsley, salt and both peppers, and simmer, stirring, for 4–5 minutes. Do not overcook the shrimp! Serve on a bed of *al dente* pasta with the sauce poured over all. Serves 6–8.

WINE: *Valpolicella or white Gavi*

Shrimp and Scallops Veronique

¾ pound shrimp, peeled and deveined
¾ pound bay scallops
½ cup heavy cream
½ cup dry vermouth
Freshly ground black pepper
3 tablespoons butter
¾ cup fish velouté or béchamel
¾ cup seedless green grapes

Heat ¼ cup heavy cream, ¼ cup vermouth and a good pinch of pepper in a 10-inch skillet. Cook until mixture is reduced to a glaze. Add the butter. When hot, add the shrimp. Stir and cook over high heat just until the shrimp turn opaque. Add the scallops and continue cooking, shaking the pan until the scallops are cooked, about 4 minutes.

With a slotted spoon, remove shrimp and scallops and keep warm. Add the remaining vermouth to the pan. Cook over high heat until the liquid is nearly evaporated. Add the velouté, stirring constantly. Add the remaining cream, still stirring, add the grapes and some more black pepper and pour sauce over shrimp and scallops. Serve over fidelini or rice pilaf. Serves 4.

Note: To make a fish velouté, add fish stock to a roux, then stir in heavy cream and a little dry sherry. For béchamel recipe, see page 150.

WINE: *White Graves or California Sauvignon Blanc*

Scallops Donna

Quick, easy, delicious.

2 pounds sea scallops (if very large, cut in half)
2 cups half-and-half
Seasoned salt and freshly ground white pepper
Flour for dredging
2 tablespoons butter
1 tablespoon chopped shallots
2 teaspoons flour
1/4 cup chicken broth
1/4 cup dry sherry
3 tablespoons heavy cream
Pinch of cayenne
Lemon wedges and parsley for garnish

Soak scallops in half-and-half for at least 30 minutes. Pat dry with paper towels and season with salt and plenty of white pepper. Dredge them in flour, shaking off excess.

Heat a large skillet and add butter. When very hot, add shallots, sauté for a minute or so and add the scallops. Shake skillet and turn scallops so they brown quickly on both sides. Do not overcook, no more than 2 minutes! Remove scallops from skillet and keep warm.

Stir 2 teaspoons flour into the residue in the skillet. Stirring all the while, add the chicken broth and sherry. Raise heat to high and reduce liquid by half.

Remove pan from heat and add the cream, stirring. Bring to a boil over high heat and reduce heat. Add a pinch of cayenne and correct seasonings. Place scallops on warm plates with sauce over. Garnish with lemon and parsley. Serves 4.

WINE: *Pouilly-Fumé*

Scallops with Saffron Beurre Blanc

The exceptional sauce is also excellent over poached fish or chicken.

SEAFOOD

24 sea scallops
Seasoned salt and freshly ground white pepper
1½ cups white wine vinegar
4 tablespoons chopped shallots
Pinch saffron threads
¼ cup heavy cream
½ pound unsalted butter, cut into pieces
Fresh lemon juice

Season the scallops with salt and pepper. Grill them just until done (opaque). Set aside and keep warm.

For the sauce: Place the vinegar and shallots in a saucepan. Cook over moderately high heat until reduced to very little liquid, a sort of glaze. Stir in the saffron and reduce further, to about 2 tablespoons. Add the cream and reduce mixture by half. Lower heat and whisk in the butter piece by piece. The butter should be absorbed into the reduction before it melts. To achieve this, you probably have to hold the pan slightly above the heat and shake it back and forth. Once the butter is completely absorbed, pour the sauce into a warm bowl and adjust the seasonings to taste with lemon juice, salt and pepper. This sauce is served more warm than hot. Spoon the sauce over the scallops and serve immediately. Serves 4–6.

WINE: *Muscadet*

Baked Stuffed Squid

Wonderful over angel-hair pasta.

3 pounds small squid, cleaned
2 cloves garlic, crushed in garlic press
2 tablespoons chopped parsley
1 cup fresh bread crumbs
½ cup Italian olive oil
1 teaspoon seasoned salt
1 teaspoon freshly ground white pepper
½ cup dry white wine

Cut off heads and tentacles from the squid and purée them in a blender or processor. Put purée in a bowl and add the garlic, parsley, bread crumbs and ¼ cup of the olive oil. Season with salt and pepper and mix well. Stuff the squid bodies with this mixture and secure it with toothpicks. Oil a large baking dish and place the squid in it. Pour the remaining oil and all the wine over the squid. Bake for 45 minutes in a 375° oven. The squid will be excellent served just as they are, with lemon juice over them, or with a light, tangy marinara sauce. Serves 6.

WINE: *Sancerre or Pinot Grigio*

Oysters Beach House

2 dozen raw oysters
1/4 cup chopped shallots
1/4 cup sliced mushrooms
1 teaspoon dry mustard
Pinch cayenne
1/2 cup butter
3/4 cup flour
2 cups milk, slightly warmed
1/2 cup dry sherry
2 egg yolks, beaten

Sauté shallots, mushrooms, mustard and cayenne in butter. Add flour and cook 3–4 minutes. Add warm milk gradually, stirring, and cook 8–10 minutes. Add sherry. Remove from fire and stir in egg yolks. Place room-temperature raw oysters in cleaned oyster shells and cover with sauce. Bake 10–12 minutes at 350°. Serves 4.

WINE: *Chablis or Muscadet*

Baked Oysters

1 pint oysters, drained
1/2 cup butter, melted
3 tablespoons chopped shallots
1 clove garlic, minced
Just over 1 cup cracker crumbs
1/2 teaspoon seasoned salt
3/4 teaspoon freshly ground black pepper
1 cup heavy cream

Butter a 1-quart baking dish. Sauté the shallots and garlic in a little butter until the garlic is opaque. Add them with the rest of the melted butter to the cracker crumbs and mix well. Season cracker crumb mixture with half the salt and pepper and mix well again. Spread half the crumbs in the baking dish and arrange the oysters over them. Season oysters with remaining salt and pepper (more if needed). Next, pour cream over all and top with remaining crumbs (a tablespoon or so of grated Parmesan can be added to crumbs for extra flavor). Bake in a preheated 375° oven for 20–25 minutes until the crumbs are nicely browned. Serves 2–4.

WINE: *Chablis or Muscadet or Greco di Tufo*

Creamed Oysters Filé

4 dozen oysters, shucked, with 1 cup of their liquor
6 cups heavy cream
½ teaspoon cayenne
Seasoned salt and freshly ground white pepper
2 tablespoons dry sherry
Juice of 1 lemon
2 teaspoons gumbo filé powder

In a heavy saucepan, reduce the cream by half over moderate heat. Strain the oyster liquor into the reduced cream and reduce the mixture to about 2½ cups. Add the cayenne, a generous pinch of white pepper, seasoned salt, sherry and lemon juice. Poach the oysters in the cream over moderate heat for about 3 minutes.

Remove the pan from the heat and stir in the filé. Serve immediately over steamed rice or serve as a soup. Either way, a little more dry sherry may be added at the last minute for extra flavor. Serves 6–8.

WINE: *Chablis or Muscadet or Fiano di Avellino*

Oysters Zia Maria

2 dozen large oysters in shells
1 clove garlic, minced
3 tablespoons butter
Salt and pepper to taste
1 cup bread crumbs
2 tablespoons Italian extra virgin olive oil
2 tablespoons chopped parsley
½ teaspoon dried oregano
Juice of 1 lemon or as needed

Scrub shells and rinse in cold running water. Insert a knife blade between edges of shells, cutting through the muscle of oyster. Remove oysters from shells.

Rub each half shell with garlic and sprinkle a little garlic on each. Next, put a tiny piece of butter over the garlic and replace the oyster. Sprinkle with salt and pepper. Mix bread crumbs, olive oil, parsley, oregano and black pepper and sprinkle this mixture atop each oyster. Arrange oysters in pan and bake in preheated 400° oven for about 10 minutes, or until oysters' edges begin to curl. Do not overcook. Squeeze lemon juice over and serve immediately. Serves 4.

WINE: *Chablis or Muscadet or Pinot Grigio*

Redfish with Oysters

4 8-ounce fillets of redfish or red snapper
24 oysters
⅓ cup dry sherry
Seasoned salt and freshly ground black pepper
Cayenne pepper
½ cup heavy cream
4 tablespoons butter, plus extra butter for baking dish and skillet
Pinch of thyme
Finely chopped fresh parsley

Open the oysters and pour their liquid into a small, heavy saucepan. If you buy jarred oysters, drain them thoroughly and use the liquor from the jar. Add sherry to the oyster liquor and reduce mixture over high heat to about 2–3 tablespoons. While mixture is reducing, preheat oven to 550° and season the fillets with seasoned salt, pepper and a pinch of cayenne. Arrange them on a buttered baking dish and drizzle lightly with sherry.

When oyster liquor and sherry are reduced, add the cream and bring mixture to a boil. Reduce the heat and whisk in the butter a little at a time to make a slightly thickened sauce. Add pinch of thyme. Remove from heat and check seasoning (a pinch of cayenne might be needed).

Keep the sauce warm while baking the fish 8–10 minutes. Be careful not to overcook the fish; it should be just barely done. While the fillets are in the oven, melt 1–2 tablespoons butter in a skillet. When butter begins to bubble, add oysters and sauté briefly, just until oysters are heated through. As soon as the fillets are done, arrange each on an individual plate, top with six oysters, then pour sauce over all, sprinkling finished dish with the parsley. Serves 4.

WINE: *Chablis or Muscadet or Gavi*

Oysters Bienville

Tony's version of an old Louisiana favorite.

3 dozen oysters on the half shell, with oyster liquor
1 bunch scallions or *2 large yellow onions, chopped very fine*
½ cup butter
2 heaping tablespoons flour
1 pint chicken or fish stock
1½ pounds boiled shrimp, cleaned and chopped very fine
1 cup mushrooms, chopped very fine
3 egg yolks
½ cup light cream or half-and-half
3 ounces white wine (Sauterne type)
Seasoned salt and freshly ground white pepper
Cayenne or Tabasco
¼ cup bread crumbs
¼ cup grated Parmesan cheese
⅛ teaspoon paprika
Lemon halves

Have 6 pie pans half-filled with rock salt. Place 6 oysters in each pan and bake in a moderate (375°–400°) oven about 10 minutes, or just until they curl around the edges. Remove and set aside. Brown scallions or yellow onions in butter until they are golden, stirring constantly. Add flour, stirring over low flame until smooth and brown. Slowly add chicken or fish stock that has been heated to the scalding (not boiling) point. Add shrimp and mushrooms and simmer until mixture begins to thicken. Set aside and allow to cool slightly.

Beat egg yolks well with cream and wine. Then, very slowly, pour the warm sauce into the egg-cream-wine mixture, stirring and beating constantly to keep smooth and prevent curdling. Add liquor from oysters and then season to taste with salt, pepper and a dash of cayenne or Tabasco sauce.

Replace on fire and cook over low flame 10–15 minutes, or until well thickened, stirring constantly. When the sauce is thick (but not too thick), spoon it carefully over individual oysters on the half shell and sprinkle each with a fairly thick covering of bread crumbs, grated cheese and paprika mixed together. Bake at 400° until tops begin to turn golden brown. Squeeze lemon juice over and serve at once. Serves 6.

WINE: *Chablis or Muscadet*

Baked Crab Cakes

These are a simple alternative to the standard fried ones. If you prefer to fry them, dip the patties into an egg-milk mixture, then in Italian-style bread crumbs and fry in butter or oil.

2 pounds cooked lump crabmeat
1 cup cubed, trimmed, soft white bread
2 teaspoons minced fresh parsley
2 teaspoons finely minced scallions (green parts only)
Pinch of thyme
Pinch of cayenne
Seasoned salt and freshly ground white pepper
1/3 cup mayonnaise
1 tablespoon Dijon or creole mustard
1 teaspoon Worcestershire sauce
Paprika
2 tablespoons butter, melted

Preheat oven to 400°. Lightly grease baking sheet. Mix bread, parsley, scallions and seasonings in a large bowl. Gently fold in crabmeat. Blend mayonnaise, mustard and Worcestershire sauce in a small bowl. Gently fold in crab mixture. Shape into 8 patties. Arrange on prepared baking sheet. Brush well with butter, and sprinkle with paprika. Bake until lightly browned, about 10–12 minutes. Serve immediately. Serves 4.

Note: Old Bay Seasoning goes particularly well in this recipe in place of the seasoned salt, as does a generous dash of both peppers.

WINE: *White Châteauneuf-du-Pape or Chardonnay*

Crabmeat au Gratin

First, make the béchamel sauce:

SEAFOOD

2 tablespoons butter
2 tablespoons flour
2 cups heavy cream
1 tablespoon dry sherry
Seasoned salt and freshly ground white pepper

In a heavy saucepan, melt the butter and stir in the flour. Over medium-low heat, stir and cook until mixture becomes foamy (do not let it color). Stir in the cream and bring to a boil, then turn fire down to a simmer. Add the sherry, stirring occasionally. Add salt and pepper to taste. (A little grated Parmesan or Gruyère may be added to the sauce, in which case it becomes a Mornay sauce rather than a béchamel.) Makes 2 cups.

Now, prepare the crab:

2 cups lump crabmeat
1 cup béchamel sauce
5 tablespoons freshly grated Romano or Parmesan cheese
Cayenne pepper
Additional salt and white pepper
4 level tablespoons grated fresh mozzarella

Gently blend the crabmeat, 1 cup of béchamel, 1 tablespoon grated Romano, pinch of cayenne, salt and white pepper. Spoon this into 4 lightly greased ramekins or ovenproof dishes.

Combine the remaining Romano and mozzarella and sprinkle over the crabmeat. Bake in a preheated 400° oven until hot. Then place under a very hot broiler for a minute, or until the top begins to brown. Serves 4.

WINE: *California Chardonnay or Fumé Blanc*

Lobster with Marsala and Vermouth

An impressive dish with many variations; Tony recommends this recipe for very important occasions.

4 ¾-pound lobster tails
¼ cup finely chopped yellow onion
2 cups dry white vermouth
½ cup dry Marsala wine
2 cups heavy cream
4 egg yolks
Seasoned salt and freshly ground black pepper
Cayenne pepper
½ cup unsalted butter, softened
1 cup Italian olive oil

Heat the grill or broiler until very hot. Place onion along with vermouth and Marsala in a saucepan. Bring to a boil and cook until the wines are almost completely evaporated. In another pan, simmer cream until it is reduced by two-thirds. When cream has partially reduced, add 2 tablespoons of it to the egg yolks and mix. Combine onion-vermouth mixture, reduced cream and egg yolk-cream mixture in top of double-boiler. Season with ½ teaspoon salt, ¼ teaspoon black pepper and ½ teaspoon cayenne. Cook over boiling water, adding the butter bit by bit and beating constantly with a wire whisk until thickened. Correct seasoning. Remove from heat and keep warm.

Wash lobster tails and split in half lengthwise. Season with additional salt and black pepper, brush with olive oil, and place shell-side-down on a very hot grill or under a very hot broiler. Grill or broil for 20–25 minutes; do not overcook. Either way, brush frequently with olive oil. Serve immediately with sauce spooned over. This sauce is also excellent with grilled scampi or warmed crabmeat. Serves 4.

WINE: *White Rhône, perhaps Crozes-Hermitage, or Gavi dei Gavi*

Poultry

. . . poultry is for the cook what canvas is for a painter.
BRILLAT-SAVARIN

Cooking is inseparable from dining, yet the first word is often perceived as a peasant and the second as an aristocrat. Sybil Ryall, in *A Fiddle For Eighteen Pence*, puts the word in its place: "Cookery, the most selfless of all arts because the least enduring, a bite or two, a little gulp and a beautiful work of thought and love is no more." She calls it art. And if Brillat-Savarin is right in his comment, quoted above, that poultry is the canvas of the artistic cook, then in the recipes that follow, there is ample opportunity for our readers to paint their masterpieces.

The majority of the poultry recipes are for *pollo*—chicken. This bird, too, is often perceived as a peasant, but we all know it can be lifted to the level of an aristocrat. Tony says, that to begin with, it must be a very fresh bird. "The perfect cooking chicken is four pounds in size, but it is often hard to find," he says. So his recipes' ingredients are scaled, realistically, to the 3- to 3½-pound chicken.

"My favorite roasting chicken is the cacklebird," says Tony. This tender bird is a desexed hen bred specifically for roasting. It usually weighs about 6 pounds and, of course, costs more than ordinary chickens. It is more common on the East Coast, but is often available elsewhere in the better meat markets.

In any case, cooks should buy only whole birds, advises Tony. Remove all visible fat and excess or loose skin, and clean the cavity thoroughly. Wash the chicken in cold water, drain it, and pat it dry. Then go directly to your favorite chicken recipe.

. . . what canvas is for a painter.

Chicken Cutlets Zingara

This dish is very popular at Tony's.

POULTRY

3 whole skinned chicken breasts, cut into halves and pounded thin (about 1/4 inch)
Seasoned salt and freshly ground white pepper
2 eggs, beaten
2 cups Italian-style bread crumbs
4 tablespoons butter
1/2 cup olive oil
2 tablespoons minced shallots
2 large cloves garlic, minced
1/2 cup Marsala
1/2 cup balsamic vinegar
1 1/2 cups demiglace or veal stock*
1/2 cup julienne strips of prosciutto
1/2 cup pitted black olives, sliced into halves
3/4 cup very ripe fresh tomatoes, peeled, seeded and chopped

Season the cutlets well on both sides with the salt and pepper. Dip them into the beaten eggs and then the bread crumbs.

In a large heavy skillet, heat the butter and olive oil. When hot, add the cutlets a few at a time (do not crowd) and sauté for about 2 minutes on each side (do not overcook). Remove cutlets from pan and keep warm. Pour out all but about a tablespoon of the grease and return pan to medium fire and add the shallots. Sauté, stirring, for 1 minute and add the garlic, stirring until the garlic becomes opaque. At this point, add the Marsala and balsamic vinegar and reduce, scraping the pan all the while until liquid is about half the original amount. Add the demiglace and when hot, add prosciutto, olives and tomatoes; stir and simmer for 2–3 minutes. Spoon this over cutlets and serve immediately.

*Classic demiglace is a complicated derivative of espagnole sauce which home cooks do not need to deal with as a rule. "Home cooks may prudently pass," Tony says. "Use a good canned or bottled brown sauce at home, but be sure it is not too salty."

WINE: *Côtes-du-Rhône-Villages, such as Gigondas, or a hearty Chianti*

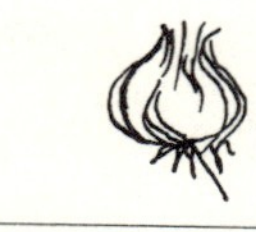

Chicken Pillows

This recipe also works well with veal cutlets.

2 whole chicken breasts, halved, skinned, boned and pounded lightly
1 garlic clove, halved
1 teaspoon dried sage
Freshly ground black pepper
2 ounces prosciutto (sliced paper-thin and fat trimmed off)
2 ounces fontina or Mascarpone, sliced thin
4 tablespoons Marsala
1 tablespoon balsamic vinegar
4 tablespoons butter
Seasoned salt
2 tablespoons parsley, chopped

Preheat oven to 350°. Lightly grease a small, shallow baking dish.

Rub chicken breasts with cut garlic clove. Next, sprinkle the breast with a pinch of sage and then pepper. Place prosciutto and then cheese over chicken. (Prosciutto slice should be smaller than cheese slice.) Roll the chicken up, starting at broader end, and secure with toothpicks. Place in baking dish. Combine Marsala, balsamic vinegar and butter and warm slightly. Pour over the chicken, then season chicken with salt and more pepper to taste. Bake until chicken is done, 20–25 minutes. (Do not overcook.) Sprinkle with parsley and serve immediately. Serves 4.

WINE: *Chianti or Brunello*

Tony's Chicken and Sausage

1 3½-pound chicken, cut up
Seasoned salt and freshly ground black pepper
4 links Italian sausage, sliced
2 tablespoons butter
2 tablespoons Italian olive oil
1 small yellow onion, finely chopped
4 cloves garlic, chopped
2 cups raw rice
3 cups boiling chicken stock
3–4 ripe tomatoes, peeled, seeded and chopped
½ pound fresh mushrooms, sliced
1 tablespoon chopped fresh parsley

Season chicken with salt and pepper and brown chicken and sausage in butter and olive oil. Pour out excess grease. Add the onion, stirring. After 4 minutes add the garlic, stirring occasionally. Add the rice, still stirring, and cook until translucent. Add boiling stock and cover; simmer for 15 minutes. Place this mixture in a buttered casserole, add the tomatoes and toss well. Bake in a preheated 375° oven for 25–30 minutes, or until the rice is cooked. Stir in the mushrooms and parsley and serve. (The mushrooms will cook from the steam of the rice.) Serves 4.

WINE: *Nuits-St.-Georges or Volnay or Barolo*

Whole Roast Chicken with Potatoes

1 3- to 3½-pound chicken
6 large cloves garlic, halved
2 teaspoons seasoned salt
½ teaspoon freshly ground black pepper
½ teaspoon dried sage
¼ teaspoon dried rosemary
4 large potatoes, peeled and cubed
2 tablespoons unsalted butter
2 tablespoons Italian extra virgin olive oil
2 tablespoons balsamic vinegar

Rub the chicken inside and out with garlic cloves, leaving 4 pieces inside the cavity. Next, rub the chicken well inside and out with a mixture of 2 teaspoons salt, ½ teaspoon (or more) black pepper, ½ teaspoon dried sage and ¼ teaspoon dried rosemary. Reserve a little of this seasoning mixture.

Preheat oven to 350° and place chicken in a roasting pan and surround with cubed potatoes. Mix melted butter and olive oil together and drizzle over the potatoes. Place the remaining garlic cloves on the potatoes. Next, sprinkle potatoes with the remaining mixture of seasonings.

Roast in oven about 35–40 minutes per pound. When chicken is about halfway done, add the balsamic vinegar, drizzling over chicken and potatoes. Chicken is done when drumsticks are tender and the juices run clear when pricked deep by a fork. Place chicken on a serving platter surrounded by the potatoes and serve with a gravy made from the pan juices. Serves 4.

WINE: *Gewürztraminer or Frascati*

Chicken with Red and Yellow Peppers

3 pounds frying chicken pieces
3 cloves garlic, crushed in a garlic press
1 cup dry white vermouth
1/3 cup brandy
2 red and 2 yellow sweet peppers, seeded and cut into strips
3/4 cup olive oil
Seasoned salt and freshly ground black pepper
Flour
1/2 cup chopped red onion
6–8 tomatoes, peeled, seeded, drained and chopped
1 1/2 tablespoons chopped fresh basil

Put the garlic in a small bowl with the wine and brandy and allow to stand for 1 hour. Gently sauté the pepper strips in 4 tablespoons of the oil in a frying pan over medium heat for 8–10 minutes. Remove from heat and set aside.

Season the chicken well with the seasoned salt and pepper and then dredge in flour. Heat 1/2 cup of the oil (or more if needed) in a large frying pan and brown the chicken, a few pieces at a time, on both sides. When all are browned, return only the legs and thighs to the pan and cover tightly. Reduce heat and simmer 10 minutes. Add the breasts and wings and simmer 10 more minutes. Transfer chicken pieces to a hot serving platter and keep warm. Pour off all but 2 tablespoons of the oil in the pan, and add the onion, cooking until golden. Add the garlic/wine/brandy mixture and reduce over high heat by half. Add the tomatoes and basil. Season with seasoned salt and a good deal of fresh pepper and simmer for 15 minutes. Return the chicken pieces to the pan and simmer for 5 minutes. Rearrange the chicken on the serving platter, pour the sauce over and top with the mixed strips of peppers. Serves 6.

WINE: *Sancerre or Chablis or California Chardonnay*

Braised Chicken Tarragon

1 3-pound chicken
1 large bunch fresh tarragon
3 tablespoons butter
3–4 ounces chicken broth
1/4 cup cognac
1/4 cup balsamic vinegar
2 1/2 cups heavy cream
Salt and freshly ground white pepper
Parsley and tarragon for garnish

Season the cavity of the chicken with the salt and pepper, then stuff with fresh tarragon. Rub the skin of the chicken with salt and pepper. Then lightly brown chicken in butter in a large pot. Add the broth, cognac, balsamic vinegar, neck, wing tips and gizzards. Cover the pot and simmer over medium-low heat for 45 minutes. Do not let juices in the pot burn. (Add more broth if needed.) Pierce the leg joint of the chicken; when done, juices will run clear. If done, remove the chicken to a warm plate, if not done, cook longer.

After the chicken has been removed, boil the liquid in the pot until it has almost all evaporated. Add the cream and a few twists of white pepper, and simmer for 10 minutes over medium-low heat. Strain. Cut the breasts, thighs and legs from the chicken and serve over steamed rice with some sauce over all. Garnish with fresh tarragon and fresh parsley. Serves 4.

WINE: *Sancerre or Pouilly-Fuissé*

Grilled Chicken

1 3- to 3½-pound chicken, cut into quarters
¾ cup fresh lemon juice
¼ cup Italian extra virgin olive oil
3–4 cloves garlic, mashed
1 teaspoon dried oregano
1 teaspoon chopped fresh parsley
Seasoned salt and freshly ground black pepper

In a bowl large enough to hold the chicken, combine lemon juice, olive oil, garlic, oregano, parsley, seasoned salt and pepper to taste. Marinate the chicken at least 3 hours, or as much as 8 hours, turning the chicken and mixing the marinade every so often.

Preheat the grill. Lay a piece of aluminum foil on grill and brush with oil. Grill chicken about 10–12 minutes per side (depending on heat and closeness to flame). Do not overcook! Brush chicken with marinade every 5 minutes during cooking. Serves 4.

WINE: *A dry white (Chablis) or a dry red (Beaujolais-Villages or Brouilly)*

Breast of Chicken Nonna

Risotto goes well with this dish.

4 whole breasts of chicken, boned
Seasoned salt and freshly ground black pepper
6 tablespoons butter
1/4 cup cognac
1 1/3 cups heavy cream
1 tablespoon meat glaze or gravy (demiglace)
2 tablespoons sherry
1 16-ounce can whole peeled tomatoes
2 cloves garlic (small to medium), minced
2 tablespoons extra virgin Italian olive oil
1 tablespoon parsley
1/4 teaspoon oregano

Salt and pepper the chicken breasts, and sauté them in a heavy skillet with 2 tablespoons butter until browned. Remove and set chicken aside, but keep warm. Add cognac to skillet, heat and ignite. Pour in cream and meat glaze and simmer 5 minutes. Add sherry, heat and pour over chicken. Garnish the center of each breast with a spoonful (not too much) of sautéed tomato mixture.

To make tomato mixture: Open can of tomatoes, discarding juice. Chop tomatoes but save the juice that collects as you chop tomatoes. Put tomato pieces and juice in skillet with garlic and olive oil and sauté for 1–2 minutes. Add parsley and a pinch of oregano and sauté another minute or so. Add salt and pepper to taste. Serves 4.

WINE: *Gavi or Pinot Grigio*

Lina's Baked Chicken Molica

This is traditionally a Sunday favorite in Italian families.

POULTRY

1 large chicken, cut into pieces (or pieces of choice)
2/3 cup freshly made dry bread crumbs
2/3 cup grated Parmesan cheese
1 teaspoon dried oregano
1/3 cup minced fresh parsley
1/2 teaspoon seasoned salt
1 teaspoon freshly ground black pepper
Pinch of cayenne
3 cloves garlic, minced
1/3 cup Italian olive oil

Mix bread crumbs, cheese, oregano, parsley, salt, pepper and cayenne in a 1-quart mixing bowl. Set aside. In a 1-quart saucepan, heat garlic and olive oil over low heat until a little more than warm. Remove from heat. Coat chicken with olive oil/garlic mixture. Then, thoroughly coat the chicken with the bread crumb mixture. Place well-coated chicken on a large ungreased cookie sheet, skin side up (skin from chicken may be removed in the beginning if desired). Mix together any remaining bread crumb mixture and olive oil mixture and sprinkle over the chicken. Bake for 1 hour and 15 minutes in a preheated 350° oven. Serves 4–6.

WINE: *Chianti*

Chicken Saltimbocca

6 whole chicken breasts, halved, skinned and boned
Freshly ground black pepper
Dried sage
12 small slices prosciutto
12 thin slices fontina or Gruyère cheese
1/4 cup all-purpose flour
2 eggs, lightly beaten
1 cup dry Italian-style bread crumbs
2 tablespoons freshly grated Romano or Parmesan cheese
1 teaspoon dried tarragon
4 tablespoons butter
1 cup chicken stock or canned broth
1 cup dry sherry
1 tablespoon cornstarch dissolved in 1 tablespoon water

Preheat oven to 400°. Place each half chicken-breast between sheets of wax paper and pound lightly to flatten. Sprinkle each breast with black pepper and a little sage, then place on each a slice of prosciutto (about 3/4 the lengths of the breast) and a slice of cheese. Roll up lengthwise and close with toothpicks.

Dip chicken rolls in flour and shake off excess. Next, dip in beaten eggs. Mix bread crumbs, cheese and tarragon, then roll the chicken breasts in this mixture. Brown rolls in butter on all sides. Transfer to a baking dish and pour chicken stock and sherry over the rolls. Bake uncovered for 25–30 minutes. Remove chicken rolls and keep warm. Drain juices into a saucepan and bring to a boil. Blend in cornstarch mixture, stirring constantly until thickened. Spoon over chicken and serve. Makes 12 serving pieces.

Note: Serving the individual chicken pieces on a bed of freshly cooked spinach makes an attractive dish.

WINE: *Frascati*

Stuffed Chicken Normandy

Tony: "This is an outstanding apple-stuffed chicken with a cider sauce. It is not as hard to prepare as it looks, and it is very much worth the effort."

4 whole chicken breasts with the first joint of the wings attached; halved, boned and skinned
½ cup minced shallots
¼ cup unsalted butter
1 Golden Delicious apple, peeled, cored and chopped
1½ teaspoons minced fresh sage leaves or *½ teaspoon dried*
1½ teaspoons minced fresh thyme leaves or *½ teaspoon dried*
Seasoned salt and freshly ground black pepper
2 teaspoons fresh lemon juice
Flour for dredging
2 large eggs, beaten with 2 teaspoons water
½ cup fine dry bread crumbs
½ cup finely chopped salted cashews
¼ cup vegetable oil

For the sauce:

½ cup minced onion
¾ cup dry white wine
¾ cup apple cider
1 cup chicken stock or canned chicken broth
1 cup heavy cream
2 tablespoons Calvados or apple brandy
4 fresh sage sprigs for garnish

To make the stuffing: In a skillet, cook the shallots in the butter over moderately low heat, stirring, until soft. Add the apple, sage, thyme, salt and pepper to taste, and cook the mixture, covered, for 10 minutes, or until the apple is just tender. Stir in the lemon juice and let the mixture cool completely.

"French" the chicken wing bone by scraping the meat off the bone with a sharp knife and reserving the meat for another use. (The wing bone will serve as a "rib" attached to the "chop.") Flatten the breasts between sheets of dampened wax paper until they are about ¼-inch thick.

Arrange the chicken breasts, skinned side down, on a work surface. In the center of each, mound 2 tablespoons of the apple mixture. Fold up the sides of the breasts to enclose the stuffing, forming the chicken into a "chop." Dredge the chops carefully in the flour, shaking off the excess. Dip them in the egg mixture, and dredge them in the bread crumbs combined with the cashews, patting the mixture onto the flesh. Arrange the chops on a rack set over a pan and chill them, uncovered, for at least 1 hour, or overnight, to let the crumbs dry.

In a large heavy skillet, heat the oil over moderate heat until it is hot but not smoking. In it, brown the chops, transferring them as they are browned to a baking pan, and bake them in a preheated 350° oven for 15–20 minutes. The chicken may be kept warm, covered loosely, for up to 10 minutes.

Make the sauce while the chops are baking: Pour off the fat from the skillet, add the onion, wine and cider, and boil the mixture until almost all the liquid is evaporated. Add the stock, and boil the mixture until the liquid is reduced by half. Add the cream and the Calvados, boiling the sauce until it is thickened slightly (there should be about 1⅓ cups), and strain it into a heated sauceboat. Transfer the chops, fitted with paper frills, to a heated platter, garnish them with the sage sprigs, and serve with the sauce. Serves 4.

WINE: *Sparkling Vouvray or Chardonnay*

Spicy Garlic Chicken

4 chicken half-breasts
4 chicken thighs, with bone
1 large onion, finely chopped
2 carrots, diced
2 celery stalks, diced
2 large sprigs fresh parsely, chopped
1/3 cup oil
36 cloves fresh garlic, peeled
Dry vermouth (white)
1/3 teaspoon crushed red pepper
Seasoned salt and freshly ground black pepper

Combine onions, carrots, celery and parsley in a large bowl and mix well. Remove skin from chicken pieces. In a large skillet, heat the oil and brown the chicken on both sides. Start with the thighs first as the breasts take less time. Drain the chicken pieces on paper towels.

Spread half of the vegetables and half of the garlic in a casserole. Arrange the chicken on top. Season the chicken with the crushed red pepper, salt and pepper. Cover the chicken with the rest of the vegetables and the rest of the garlic. Over the entire mixture sprinkle vermouth (enough to lightly moisten) and cover the casserole tightly. Bake for 1 hour and 30 minutes to 2 hours in a preheated 325° oven.

Eat with a lot of good French or Italian bread and use the cooked garlic to spread with a touch of butter on the crusty bread. Serves 4–6.

WINE: *With a dish calling for 36 garlic cloves, Dewey urges "a big, spicy monster—a Côte Rôtie," one of the finest Rhone reds, or Amarone.*

Breast of Chicken Sauté with Curry

Be sure to use a fresh, good-quality curry mixture for this dish.

3 pounds chicken breast, cut into 1½-inch pieces
Seasoned salt and freshly ground black pepper
Flour for dredging
2 tablespoons butter
3 tablespoons Italian olive oil
2 tablespoons curry powder
¾ cup dry white wine
¼ cup brandy
6 whole tomatoes (imported canned tomatoes, drained)
2 apples, peeled and sliced
⅓ cup pitted green olives, sliced
Bouquet garni: 3 sprigs parsley and 2 sprigs thyme (or ½ teaspoon dried)

Season the breast pieces with salt and pepper and dredge in flour, shaking off excess. Heat butter and olive oil in a large heavy skillet over a fairly high heat. Sauté the chicken for about 2 minutes on each side. When the chicken is fully cooked (do not overcook), remove and keep warm.

Drain off all but 2 tablespoons of fat from the pan, add the curry powder and stir for 1 minute over medium heat. Add the wine and reduce by half. Heat the brandy in a ladle over medium heat, ignite and add to the pan. Add the whole tomatoes, apples, olives and bouquet garni. Season with salt and an extra pinch of pepper; simmer for 8–10 minutes. Return chicken to pan, simmer for 3–5 minutes longer. Remove bouquet garni and serve chicken and sauce immediately. Rice is a natural accompaniment for this dish. Serves 6.

WINE: *Chablis or a big Chardonnay*

Chicken Breasts with Green Peppercorns

4 large whole chicken breasts, halved, skinned and boned
8 tablespoons butter
3 tablespoons green peppercorns
4 tablespoons cognac
1 cup chicken stock or canned broth
2 tablespoons minced shallots
1 small garlic clove, minced
2 tablespoons flour
½ cup dry white wine
¾ cup heavy cream
3 egg yolks
Seasoned salt and freshly ground black pepper

Preheat oven to 350°. Make a paste of 2 tablespoons butter and 1 tablespoon green peppercorns. Flatten chicken breasts slightly and make a slit in the thick side to form a small pocket. Brush breasts with about 1 tablespoon of the cognac and place a scant 1 teaspoon of the paste in the pocket of each breast.

In a large skillet heat 4 tablespoons of the butter and slowly brown the breasts on each side. When all are done, remove to a serving platter and keep warm. Drain off all but 1 tablespoon of the butter from the skillet and add remaining cognac to deglaze the pan. Stir and warm the cognac, then ignite to burn off the alcohol. Add pan juices to the chicken stock and set aside.

Melt remaining 2 tablespoons of the butter in the skillet, add shallots and garlic and sauté briefly (about 1 minute). Sprinkle with flour, cooking and stirring for 3 minutes. Slowly add chicken stock and wine. Stir and cook until the sauce is smooth and thickened.

In a small bowl, beat together the cream and egg yolks. Add a tablespoon or two of the warm sauce, mix, then slowly pour cream and yolks into the skillet. Add remaining 2 tablespoons of the green peppercorns and correct seasoning. Pour sauce over chicken and reheat all in the oven for 5–10 minutes and serve with rice or noodles. Serves 6–8.

WINE: *Monbazillac, a white, semisweet Dordogne wine, or California Chardonnay.*

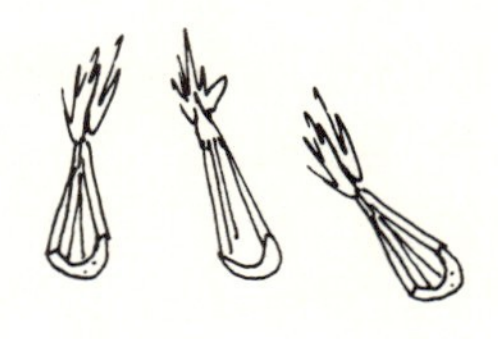

Plum Blossom Chicken

6 large whole chicken breasts, halved
2 tablespoons butter
1 teaspoon curry powder
½ cup plum jam
¼ cup cream sherry or medium sherry
1 tablespoon fresh lemon juice
1 lemon, thinly sliced

In a heavy skillet, brown chicken breasts in butter. Stir curry into pan juices. Blend plum jam, sherry and lemon juice and pour over chicken. Cover each breast with a slice or two of lemon. Cover skillet and simmer for 30–35 minutes. Remove chicken to heated platter and keep warm. Boil pan juices to reduce slightly. Spoon over chicken and serve immediately. Serves 6.

WINE: *An Oregon or Washington state Riesling*

Chicken Aiello

1 fryer, cut up (3½ pounds)
Seasoned salt and freshly ground black pepper
¼ cup Italian olive oil
1 cup peas, fresh or frozen
¼ cup sliced black olives
2 peppers, 1 red and 1 yellow, seeded and cut into strips
1 red onion, thinly sliced and chopped
4–5 cloves garlic, minced
2 carrots, shredded
3–4 large red ripe tomatoes, peeled, seeded and chopped
1 cup dry white wine
1½ teaspoons fresh or *½ teaspoon each dried rosemary, thyme and basil*

Wash and pat the chicken dry, and season well with the salt and pepper. Heat the olive oil and brown the chicken pieces on all sides in a large skillet or Dutch oven.

Except for the peas and olives, add the remaining ingredients, cover, and simmer for 30 minutes, or until the chicken is tender. Stir in the peas and olives and simmer for 5–10 minutes more. Skim off the excess fat and serve chicken over buttered pasta or rice or with steamed new potatoes. (New potatoes may also be added to this dish.) Serves 4.

WINE: *A red Bandol, a Provençal wine, which Andre Crispin describes as "made to order for this dish," or Chablis*

From top, *Baked Ziti With Sausage and Ricotta, Linguine Alle Vongole and Pasta Pizzaiola*

Braised Chicken with Saffron

2 fryers, 2–3 pounds each, cut up
Seasoned salt and freshly ground black pepper
Paprika
1/3 cup olive oil
1 large red onion, chopped
2 red and 2 yellow peppers, seeded and sliced
4 cloves garlic, minced
2 16-ounce cans chopped Italian tomatoes with juice
1 cup chicken stock or canned broth
1 bay leaf
1/2 teaspoon saffron threads
1 1/2 teaspoons fresh or *1/2 teaspoon each dried thyme, basil and oregano*
12 pitted and quartered green olives
12 pitted and quartered black olives
1/2 cup dry Marsala or red wine

Sprinkle the chicken pieces with seasoned salt, pepper and paprika. In a large skillet or Dutch oven, heat the oil and brown the chicken on all sides. Remove the chicken and set aside. Add the onion, peppers and garlic to the drippings and sauté for 5 minutes. Add the tomato, stock and remaining ingredients. Bring to a boil, lower the heat, and simmer for 5 minutes. Add the chicken pieces, cover, and simmer until the chicken is tender, about 35–45 minutes. Season to taste with seasoned salt and a good pinch of pepper. Serve with rice or buttered noodles. Serves 6–8.

WINE: *Nebbiolo or Gattinara*

Chicken Saltimbocca served on a bed of spinach

Baked Chicken with Porcini and Capers

2 whole chickens, cut up
8 tablespoons butter
Seasoned salt and freshly ground black pepper
2–3 large cloves garlic, minced
1 tablespoon fresh parsley, chopped
½ teaspoon dried rosemary
½ teaspoon crushed red pepper flakes
Pinch of ginger
Juice of 1 lemon
6 pieces porcini mushrooms, washed, chopped and presoaked in a cup of dry sherry
8–10 fresh mushrooms, sliced
2 tablespoons balsamic vinegar
1 tablespoon capers, rinsed

In 1 or 2 large baking dishes, break up butter into small chunks. Arrange chicken on butter. Skin side up, season with salt and pepper. Sprinkle the garlic over the chicken. Bake uncovered in a preheated 350° oven until the butter melts. Baste the chicken and add herbs and spices, being careful to distribute the pepper flakes evenly. Bake, basting often, for 10 minutes. Squeeze lemon over all, baste again and cook 3 minutes. Add porcini and sherry and cook, basting, another 10 minutes. Add fresh mushrooms and balsamic vinegar and cook another 10 minutes, basting. Add capers and cook another 5–8 minutes, basting. Chicken should be nicely browned. Serve with sauce spooned over chicken and with a little more fresh chopped parsley. Serves 6–8.

WINE: *Brunello*

Broiled Poussin

A poussin is a very young chicken weighing about 1¼ pounds.

4 poussins, cut in half
6 cloves garlic, minced
2 teaspoons dried thyme
Fruity Italian olive oil
Seasoned salt and freshly ground black pepper
3 tablespoons chopped parsley
4 lemon halves

Lay the hen halves flat and ease the skin away from the breast with a small sharp knife, and push minced garlic and dried thyme underneath. Brush both sides of the poussin halves with olive oil and season all over with the salt and black pepper. Heat the broiler to a very hot stage. Brush the broiling pan with olive oil, put the poussins, skin side up, about 4–6 inches from the broiler. Broil for about 4 minutes on each side, or until cooked through and crispy (do not overcook). Arrange 2 halves on each of four warmed plates. Squeeze half a lemon over each serving and sprinkle fresh chopped parsley over. Serve immediately with lemon wedges on the side. Serves 4.

WINE: *Barbaresco*

Poussin in Honey Sauce with Figs

4 poussins, cut in half
2 tablespoons olive oil
1/2 cup chopped onion
3–4 cloves garlic, crushed
1 tablespoon brandy
2/3 cup dry white vermouth
1 1/4 cups chicken stock
4 tablespoons honey
2 ounces (1/3 cup) dried figs, chopped
5 tablespoons lemon juice
Bouquet garni: sprigs of thyme, parsley and a few black peppercorns
1 tablespoon butter, softened
1 tablespoon flour
4 fresh figs, quartered
Seasoned salt and freshly ground black pepper

Heat the oil in a large flameproof casserole, add the poussins and brown all over. Remove from pan and set aside. Sauté the onion and garlic in the oil until soft, then stir in the brandy and wine. Increase the heat and bring to a boil. Return the poussins to the casserole, then add the stock, honey, dried figs, lemon juice and bouquet garni. Cover and simmer over low heat for about 1 hour and 15–30 minutes. Remove the poussins from the pan and keep hot.

Strain the cooking liquid into a saucepan. Mix the softened butter and flour together well and beat into the sauce a little at a time. Simmer gently for 5 minutes. Add salt and pepper and a little wine if desired. Add the fresh figs and simmer for 2 minutes. Pour sauce over poussins and serve immediately. Serves 4.

WINE: *Arbois, a Jura wine known as "vin jaune" (yellow, or straw, wine), or Château-Chalon (a village), another Jura wine (Crispin: "The only white wine in the world that must never be chilled") or Meursault.*

Truffle Capon

1 5–6 pound capon or cacklebird
2 tablespoons seasoned salt and freshly ground black pepper
1½ teaspoons poultry seasoning
2 truffles, sliced thin (if canned, add juice also)
1 large red onion, quartered
2 cloves garlic, halved
½ cup dry sherry
½ cup cognac
1 tablespoon butter

Season the capon inside and out with the salt, pepper and poultry seasoning. Carefully loosen the skin from the breast meat and drumsticks. Do not break the skin. Slip a truffle slice or two on top of each drumstick and arrange at least 12 slices of truffle in 2 parallel rows down the breast bone.

Put onion quarters, garlic, sherry, cognac and butter in the bottom of a roasting pan and place the capon on top. Roast the capon in a preheated 400° oven and allow 18–20 minutes per pound. Baste the bird every 15 minutes. When the capon is done, a variety of sauces can be made from the pan juices. One excellent variation is to add ½ cup of balsamic vinegar and ¼ cup demiglace the last 20 minutes. Serves 4–5.

WINE: *A Château Gruaud-Larose (a St. Julien) or Brunello*

Cranberry-stuffed Game Hens

4 game hens, fresh if possible (or *any 1- to 2-pound small bird, such as Rock Cornish hen, squab, poussin or baby hen)*
3 cups stale bread cubes
Seasoned salt and freshly ground white pepper
1 teaspoon sage
1/2 teaspoon dried thyme
1/4 teaspoon dried oregano or marjoram
1/4 pound bacon, chopped
1 medium onion, chopped
1/4 cup chopped celery
1 clove garlic, chopped
1/2 cup cranberries, fresh or frozen
1/3 cup chopped pecans
1 6-ounce can frozen orange juice concentrate, thawed
3/4 cup water
1 teaspoon sugar
1 teaspoon aromatic bitters or Campari

To prepare the stuffing, toast the bread cubes in a 300° oven for 30 minutes or until hard and brown. In a small bowl, toss the browned cubes with seasoned salt to taste, a good pinch of white pepper, and herbs, and set aside.

Preheat oven to 400°. Wash the hens under cold running water and pat dry. Sprinkle the birds inside and out with seasoned salt and pepper.

In a heavy skillet over medium heat, sauté the bacon until crisp. Remove bacon and drain on paper towels. In a little of the bacon fat, sauté the onion and celery over medium heat for 5 minutes, then add the garlic and cook another 2 minutes. Remove skillet from heat and stir in cranberries, pecans and bread-herb mixture.

In a small bowl mix the orange juice concentrate, water, sugar and the bitters. Pour half of this mixture into the cranberry stuffing and reserve the rest for basting the birds.

Stir the stuffing until it is well blended and all the liquid is absorbed. Fill each bird cavity and sew or skewer the openings, and tie the legs together.

Put the stuffed birds on a rack in a shallow roasting pan. Roast in the middle of the oven for 1 hour, or until birds are tender. Baste well with the orange juice mixture every 10–15 minutes.

Remove the birds to a warm platter and serve with the pan juices spooned over them. Serves 4.

WINE: *Vouvray*

Whole Roast Duckling with Pine Nuts

1 duckling (4–5 pounds)
Seasoned salt and freshly ground black pepper
2 cups demiglace
Juice of 2 lemons
Orange juice concentrate (about 1 tablespoon)
Red wine
Parsley, freshly chopped
Pine nuts, browned

Season duckling, inside and outside, with salt and pepper. With a fork, prick both sides of the breast a few times. Roast in a 550° oven about 45 minutes, or until well-browned and crispy.

Sauce: Heat 2 cups demiglace (canned mushroom sauce would be convenient for home use), adding the lemon juice, frozen orange juice concentrate, a touch of red wine, parsley and pine nuts. Let sauce simmer for 20 minutes and serve. You can easily correct sauce by tasting and adding more or less of any of the above. For an extra touch (and it is done at Tony's), you can add a small amount of finely chopped fresh mushrooms and scallions to the sauce. Serves 2.

WINE: *California Merlot or Saint-Émilion*

Duck with Cognac and Nectarines

1 duck (4–5 pounds)
3 ounces (½ cup) dried nectarines
Boiling water
2 tablespoons cognac
2 tablespoons port
2 tablespoons butter
½ orange
Seasoned salt and freshly ground black pepper
Dash of cinnamon
4 nectarines or peaches, pitted and sliced

Place the dried fruit in a bowl and cover with boiling water. Leave until lukewarm, then stir in cognac and port. Leave to soak overnight. Place the nectarines, the soaking liquid and the butter in a small saucepan. Cover and simmer very gently for 20 minutes, adding more port if the mixture seems too dry. Purée the fruit and reserve.

Preheat the oven to 375°. Prick the duck all over the top side with a fork. Place the orange inside the duck's cavity. Place on a rack in a roasting pan and season duck with salt and pepper. Roast for 30 minutes per pound. Remove duck from oven and discard orange. Carefully tip duck so cavity juices run into pan, then transfer duck to a plate and keep hot. Pour off fat and stir in remaining water and nectarine purée. Simmer over moderate heat for about 10 minutes, stirring in a dash of cinnamon.

Warm the sliced nectarines in the oven for 2 minutes. Carve the duck into slices and serve with nectarine slices over the duck and spoon the sauce over all. Serves 2.

WINE: *A red Hermitage or Amarone*

Pheasant in Marsala Sauce with Truffles

1 pheasant weighing 3½-4 pounds
Seasoned salt and freshly ground black pepper
1 clove garlic, sliced
Liver (optional)
¼ cup minced lean cooked ham
1 small can black truffles, sliced (save oil)
8 juniper berries, crushed
5 tablespoons olive oil
2 tablespoons butter
¾ cup dry Marsala

Season cavity by rubbing with garlic, salt and pepper. Wash liver and chop. Mix with ham. Add half the truffle slices and juniper berries. Use mixture to stuff pheasant. Sew up pheasant to hold the stuffing in, truss bird and brown in a Dutch oven in olive oil and butter for 10–12 minutes. Sprinkle outside of bird with seasoned salt and pepper. Rotate the bird often while it is browning, so it browns evenly on all sides.

Pour in Marsala and cook for 5 minutes over high heat. Sprinkle remaining truffles and any of their oil over the pheasant, cover, and lower heat. There will be a thick dark sauce forming in the pan. It will take about 40–45 minutes for the bird to cook. Prick with a fork to test if pheasant is done. If juices run clear, it's ready. Transfer to platter, spoon plenty of pan juice over and serve immediately. Serves 4.

WINE: *Gevrey-Chambertin or Barolo*

Deviled Baby Hens

4 Cornish game hens, or equivalent
Wild rice, cooked and well-seasoned
Fresh mushrooms
1 cup chicken bouillon
Paprika
Butter
Diavola sauce

Stuff game hens with seasoned rice and mushrooms. Place hens in a greased baking dish with bouillon and bake, covered, in a preheated oven at 400° for 30 minutes, or until tender. Remove hens from oven, sprinkle with a touch of paprika and coat with butter. Place under preheated broiler and brown. Make sauce.

Diavola sauce:

4 tablespoons Italian extra virgin olive oil
1 scallion, chopped
2 cloves garlic, minced
1 teaspoon finely chopped chervil or parsley
1 teaspoon cracked black pepper
½ cup brandy or sherry
1 tablespoon Worcestershire sauce
1 teaspoon dry English mustard
2–3 drops Tabasco
2 cups demiglace or brown gravy sauce
Juice of 1 lemon
2 tablespoons ketchup

Heat oil in skillet and sauté scallion, garlic and chervil or parsley. When they are soft, add all other ingredients and simmer slowly for about 10 minutes.

Pour diavola sauce over hens and serve. Serves 4.

WINE: *A red Zinfandel*

Meat

Wine is the intellectual part of a meal.
Meats are merely the material part.
ALEXANDRE DUMAS *PERE*

Beef is the soul of cooking.
MARIE-ANTOINE CAREME

AT SOME POINT in taking in all these dishes—the plain and the elegant, the down-home and the Lucullan—some may wonder if gourmandism is dangerous to their health. Perish the thought! For at least two centuries learned men have been telling us that living high on the hog is good for us, that gourmands live longer and in better health than others. In 1820, one Dr. Villermet presented a paper to the French Academy of Science in Paris in which he proved that gourmands live longer, and in the pink all the way. Jean Anthelme Brillat-Savarin, that most revered of epicures, citing the same Villermet's evidence, concluded that "good living is far from being destructive to good health . . . all things being equal, gourmands live much longer than other folk."

Writing more than a century later, Julian Street, our own Brillat-Savarin, also found gastronomy to be beneficial, but with a bit more point. "Gourmets don't get fat," he wrote. "Almost without exception, those we have known have been healthily lean, or at most what we call 'comfortably filled out.' They tend to be long-lived and in old age to appear younger than their years. . . ."

The best thing to do, as you speculate on these meat recipes with here and there a touch of Italy, is to fall back on Street's "comfortably filled out." A happy, epicurean thought; much nicer than "pudgy."

Veal Cutlets

Tony: "On one of my trips to Corleone, Sicily, my uncle and cousin butchered a calf. From that calf came light, crispy, succulent veal cutlets like these."

4 veal chops, ¾-1 inch thick, trimmed and pounded thin with bone left on or *4–6 veal scaloppine, pounded thin (Tony prefers the bone-on cutlet)*
2 eggs, beaten
1 teaspoon seasoned salt
Freshly ground white pepper to taste
¼ cup fresh bread crumbs
½ cup grated Parmesan cheese
1 tablespoon chopped fresh parsley
¼ cup flour
3 tablespoons unsalted butter
1 tablespoon Italian olive oil
4 lemon quarters

Season beaten eggs with salt and pepper. Combine bread crumbs, cheese, parsley and a pinch of pepper and mix well.

Dust the veal lightly with flour, shaking off any excess. Dip each cutlet first in egg, then in bread crumb–cheese mixture. Refrigerate for 30 minutes so the breading will adhere well.

In a skillet large enough to hold all the veal, melt butter with oil over medium heat. Sauté the chops until golden brown and tender, about 5 minutes on each side. Set on paper towels to dry, gently blotting them. Move to warm plates, squeeze lemon juice over and serve immediately. Serves 4.

WINE: *Gavi (white) or Dolcetto d'Alba (light red)*

Saltimbocca alla Romano

Saltimbocca means "jump into the mouth," implying, Waverley Root has written, "that it is so delicious that it slides down all by itself, without the exertion of willpower by the eater. . . ." The Italians describe this joining of a thin slice of veal to another of prosciutto as *maritati*—married. What a sublime marriage!

12 slices veal scaloppine
Seasoned salt and freshly ground black pepper
½ cup flour
9 tablespoons butter
¾ teaspoon chopped fresh or dried sage
12 paper-thin slices prosciutto
12 paper-thin slices fontina cheese
⅓ cup dry Marsala
3–4 tablespoons demiglace
1 teaspoon fresh chopped parsley

Season veal with salt and pepper, then dredge in flour, shaking off any excess. Heat 3 tablespoons butter in a skillet and quickly sauté the veal on each side (about 30 seconds per side). Remove the veal and pat it dry with paper towels. Sprinkle the sage lightly over the veal, then add a slice of prosciutto and a slice of cheese. Fold veal over into a cylindrical shape and "pin" with a toothpick.

Discard butter from sautéing the veal and to the pan add 6 more tablespoons butter. Melt the butter over medium heat. Season the butter with salt and pepper and a pinch of sage. When the butter sizzles, add the wine and then the demiglace. Cook for a minute or so, stirring, and add the veal, stirring and spooning the sauce over it. Sprinkle the parsley over all and stir it into the sauce. Let the meat cook in the sauce until hot and the cheese inside starts to melt (about 3–5 minutes). Remove toothpicks and serve immediately with sauce over. Serves 4–6.

WINE: *Frascati or Merlot or Sangiovese*

Veal Sauté with Leeks

MEAT

1¾ pounds boneless veal, cut from the leg
1¾ pounds leeks, white part only (about 2 bunches)
3 tablespoons butter
3 tablespoons imported peanut oil
Coarse salt
Freshly ground white pepper
½ cup dry white wine
Bouquet garni (of thyme, parsley and bay leaf)
¾ cup milk
Juice of ½ lemon

Cut the veal into 2-inch cubes, about 1½ ounces each. (This should yield approximately 4 pieces per person.) Cut the leeks into thin, even slices.

Heat the butter with the oil in a heavy copper pan or enameled cast-iron skillet large enough to hold the pieces of meat side by side. Season the veal with salt and pepper and arrange in the pan. Brown the meat, slowly, on each side, allowing about 15 minutes in all. Use tongs to turn the veal without piercing it.

Lower heat and add the leeks. Cook, covered, 10 minutes to release their juices. Stir once or twice, and make sure they do not brown. Add wine and bouquet garni, bring to a simmer, then add milk. Cook 1 hour, partially covered, stirring frequently. The sauce should thicken by itself.

Add a few drops of lemon juice. Taste for seasoning, simmer a few minutes, and serve. Serves 4.

WINE: *Pouilly-Fumé*

Vitello Tonnato with Sweet Red Pepper Sauce

3 pounds rolled leg of veal
1 teaspoon salt
1 teaspoon freshly ground black pepper
½ cup sliced red onion
1 carrot, sliced
1 stalk celery, sliced
3 sprigs parsley
2 cloves garlic
4 cups boiling water
1 7¾-ounce can tuna
2–4 sweet red peppers, roasted, peeled, cored and sliced
8 anchovy fillets
¼ cup lemon juice
¾ cup Italian extra virgin olive oil
2 tablespoons capers, rinsed and drained

Rub the veal with the salt and ½ teaspoon pepper. Place in a heavy saucepan and brown it over high heat. Pour off the fat. Add the onion, carrot, celery, parsley, garlic and boiling water. Cover and cook over low heat until tender, about 1½ hours. Drain, dry and cool.

Roast the red peppers in a broiler or over open flame until charred. Cool, then peel, core and slice.

Purée the tuna, peppers, anchovies and lemon juice in an electric blender or in a food processor. Very gradually and steadily, beat in the olive oil a little at a time until the consistency of a thin mayonnaise. Whisk in the capers.

Refrigerate the veal until very cold. When ready to serve, slice veal very thin and cover with sauce. Variation: Instead of peppers, substitute ½ cup of fresh sweet basil or a mixture of both. Serves 8–12 as an appetizer, or 4–6 as an entree.

WINE: *Gavi*

Osso Buco with Balsamic Vinegar

4 thick (1–1½ inch) veal shanks (have butcher trim off fat)
Seasoned salt and freshly ground black pepper
Flour
6–8 tablespoons Italian extra virgin olive oil
1½ cups finely chopped carrots
6–8 cloves garlic, minced
1 28-ounce can imported Italian tomatoes (juice and all)
4 tablespoons tomato paste
1 red onion, finely chopped
⅔ cup chicken stock
1 cup dry white wine
6 anchovy fillets, chopped (optional)
½ cup balsamic vinegar
3 tablespoons chopped fresh parsley

Season both sides of the veal shanks with the salt and pepper and then dredge in flour. Select a roasting pan or casserole large enough to hold the veal shanks in one layer. Heat the olive oil in the pan and brown the veal chops well on both sides (this will take about 5 minutes). Arrange the slices, bone up, in the pan. To the veal add the carrots, half the garlic, all the tomatoes, tomato paste and onion. Next, pour in the chicken stock and white wine. Stir as well as possible. Cover the pan and reduce the heat. Let simmer gently for about 2 hours. Add the anchovy fillets, the rest of the garlic and the balsamic vinegar. Correct the seasoning if needed. Stir well and let simmer 15 more minutes. Sprinkle with chopped parsley and serve immediately. Serves 4.

Note: If you don't like anchovies, leave them out, alas.

WINE: *Any big California Cabernet Sauvignon or Brunello*

Veal Maxine

Houston Chronicle columnist Maxine Mesinger won the 1982 March of Dimes Gourmet Gala using this recipe.

4 thick veal loin chops
Seasoned salt and freshly ground white pepper
¼ cup flour
3 tablespoons butter
2 teaspoons finely chopped shallots
1 10-ounce package frozen artichoke hearts, broken apart
1 teaspoon crushed green peppercorns
1 cup champagne or dry vermouth
1 cup heavy cream
3 large mushrooms, sliced into T-shapes

Sprinkle chops with salt and pepper on both sides, then dredge in flour. Melt 2 tablespoons butter in a skillet and cook the chops on both sides, browning well, about 12–15 minutes. Remove the chops to a warm place and keep warm.

To the same skillet, empty out old butter and add remaining butter and shallots (one chopped piece garlic optional). Cook briefly and add the artichoke hearts. Cook, stirring for a minute or two, then add the peppercorns and champagne and cook over high heat until the liquid is reduced to about ⅓ cup. Stir as necessary to deglaze the pan (to dissolve the brown particles that cling to the sides and bottom of the pan). Add the cream and mushrooms. Cook over high heat for about 5 minutes and correct seasoning. Pour sauce over chops and serve immediately. Serves 4.

WINE: *Beaujolais or a Swiss red (the best of which is Dôle) or Brunello*

Veal and Apple Rolls

2 sharp Granny Smith or other tart green apples, peeled, cored and finely chopped
2 cups ground veal
1 egg, beaten
1½ teaspoons sugar
Salt and freshly ground white pepper
½ cup all-purpose flour
5 tablespoons butter
¼ cup red wine

Put the apples in a bowl along with meat, egg, sugar, salt and pepper to taste. Stir well to mix, adding a little of the flour to bind the mixture. Shape the mixture into rissoles (football shapes) and coat with flour.

Melt the butter in a large frying pan, add the rissoles and fry over moderate heat until browned on all sides. Add the wine, cover and cook gently for 15 minutes more. Serve hot. Serves 2–4.

WINE: *Beaumes de Venise, a red Côtes-du-Rhône that has been called France's best dessert Muscat*

Veal Strips Sautéed in White Wine

A very simple dish. The trick is not to overcook the veal.

1¼ pounds veal scaloppine, cut into strips
2 tablespoons butter
2 tablespoons olive oil
2 cloves garlic, minced
2 bay leaves
Seasoned salt and freshly ground black pepper
¾ cup dry white wine
Pinch of crushed red pepper

Melt the butter and oil in a large skillet and add the garlic and bay leaves, and sauté gently for 2 minutes. Discard bay leaves. Season the veal with salt and pepper; add to the pan and sauté quickly until the veal is browned. Add the wine and a pinch of crushed red pepper, a dab of black pepper and seasoned salt. Boil until reduced somewhat and serve immediately over pasta or rice. Serves 4.

WINE: *The red Corbières, a thin spicy wine*

Veal Chops Parisienne

This is a very rich, very French, very delicious entree.

6 thick veal chops (trimmed of all fat), slightly pounded
Seasoned salt and freshly ground white pepper to taste
Flour for dredging
½ cup each butter and oil
½-¾ cup good port wine
1 pint heavy cream
⅓ cup demiglace
Black truffles

Salt and pepper cutlets on both sides, then dredge in flour. Heat oil and butter in a large skillet, add the veal chops and cook for 4–5 minutes on each side. Remove chops and keep warm. Add the port wine and reduce to almost dry, add the heavy cream and demiglace. Cook the sauce a few minutes and pour it on the cutlets. For the finishing touch, put a slice or two of truffle on each chop. Serves 6.

WINE: *Chambolle-Musigny*

Veal Chops with Mushroom and Mustard Sauce

4 12-ounce veal chops, trimmed
1 pound fresh mushrooms of your choice
5 tablespoons butter
2 cloves garlic, chopped
1¼ cups heavy cream
2 teaspoons creole mustard
1 teaspoon Dijon mustard
Seasoned salt and freshly ground black pepper
Lemon juice
Olive oil
Chives or scallions, chopped fine

Clean the mushrooms and sauté over moderate heat in a frying pan with a tablespoon of butter and chopped garlic. Stir with a slotted spoon for about 2 minutes, or until the mushrooms are barely done. Remove mushrooms from the pan with the slotted spoon and set aside.

Add the cream to the pan and boil for 3–4 minutes to reduce the cream sauce. Add the mustards, stir well, and add 3½ tablespoons of butter broken into small pieces. Whisk the sauce to combine well. Do not boil the sauce. Add the salt and pepper to taste and a little lemon juice.

Salt and pepper the veal. Cook it in a hot frying pan with some olive oil for about 2 minutes on each side. Then place the veal chops in a preheated 500° oven for about 10 minutes or till done (medium-rare). Place the veal chops on warm plates with some mushrooms on each one and spoon the hot sauce over all. Sprinkle the finely chopped chives or scallions over all and serve immediately. Serves 4.

WINE: *A red Zinfandel or Gewürztraminer or Chianti*

Veal Chops with Neapolitan Sauce

4 servings veal chop or your favorite steak
3 tablespoons olive oil
½ cup minced onion
3 cloves garlic, minced
1 28-ounce can tomatoes (preferably imported), well drained
2–3 tablespoons red wine
4–6 fresh basil leaves, torn
½ teaspoon oregano
1–2 tablespoons capers (preferably Italian), drained
¼ cup oil-cured black olives, cut in halves
Seasoned salt and freshly ground black pepper

Heat olive oil in skillet and add onions, sautéing over medium heat 4–5 minutes. Stir in garlic and sauté for 1 minute more. Increase heat and add tomatoes, wine, basil and oregano and boil 4–5 minutes only. Quickly mix in capers and olives. Correct seasoning with seasoned salt and generous pinch of black pepper. Pour over rare steaks or chops and serve immediately. Serves 4.

WINE: *A Neapolitan red or Amarone*

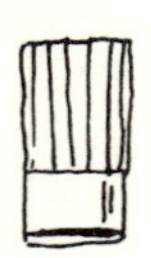

Veal Chops with Rosemary and Vermouth

4 rib veal chops, 1 inch thick
Seasoned salt and freshly ground black pepper
Flour for dredging
6 tablespoons butter
1 cup dry white vermouth or white wine
2 cloves garlic, crushed in the garlic press
½ teaspoon dried rosemary or *1 teaspoon chopped fresh*
2 tablespoons demiglace or brown sauce
Juice of ½ lemon

Season the chops well with the salt and pepper. Dredge with flour, shaking off excess. Heat 4 tablespoons butter in a large heavy skillet until hot. Add chops and brown on each side for 3 minutes. Remove chops. Add the wine to the pan and reduce over high heat. Return chops to the pan (overlapping each other if necessary). Sprinkle the garlic and rosemary over each chop and grind the peppermill again over the chops.

Cover the pan and simmer over very low heat for 15–20 minutes. Turn chops once during simmering and baste with juices in the pan. Transfer chops to a serving platter and keep warm. Add the demiglace to the juices in the pan and reduce over high heat to ½-¾ cup. Remove from heat, add lemon juice and swirl in remaining butter, bit by bit. Spoon sauce over chops and serve at once. (Variation: Add porcini or other mushrooms.) Serves 4.

WINE: *A red Zinfandel or Brunello*

Veal Medallions

4 medallions of veal, 6 ounces each, or *8 medallions, 3 ounces each (medallions are cut from the veal loin and are rather thick)*
Seasoned salt and freshly ground white pepper
Flour
2 tablespoons cooking oil
1/4 cup unsalted butter, cut into small pieces
1 shallot, chopped fine
1 small garlic clove, chopped fine
2 tablespoons brandy
1/4 cup demiglace or mushroom sauce
1/4 cup heavy cream

With the palm of your hand, flatten veal slightly. Season with salt and pepper. Dust lightly with flour, shaking off any excess. In a heavy skillet large enough to hold the veal, heat the oil. Over very high heat, brown the veal medallions about 30 seconds on each side.

Discard oil, lower heat and add the butter, shallot and garlic to pan. Cook for 1–2 minutes. Pour in brandy and ignite it. Flame will only last a few seconds. Add brown sauce and cream and continue cooking until medallions are medium-rare, about 4–5 minutes for 6-ounce medallions, 2–3 minutes for 3-ounce. Season with salt and pepper. Serve immediately on heated plate with sauce spooned over. Serves 4.

Variation: Stir in slightly cooked asparagus tips when you add the medallions at the last stage of cooking.

WINE: *Saint-Émilion*

Medallions of Veal in Port Sauce with Ginger

16 (3–4 ounce) veal medallions, cut ¾-inch thick
Seasoned salt and freshly ground black pepper
2 tablespoons oil
4 tablespoons unsalted butter

Sauce:

1 cup port
3 cups brown stock or sauce
2 teaspoons freshly grated ginger or to taste
½ teaspoon Dijon mustard
Salt and freshly ground black pepper

To prepare veal, season each medallion on both sides with salt and pepper. Heat oil and 1 tablespoon butter in large skillet over medium-high heat. Add veal and sauté until medium-rare, about 1–2 minutes. Transfer to platter and keep warm.

To prepare port sauce, discard any fat in skillet. Add port to skillet, scraping up any browned bits. Place over medium-high heat and reduce to syrupy glaze. Stir in brown sauce, ginger and mustard and reduce by half, stirring constantly. Strain into saucepan and cook over medium heat 1 minute. Whisk in remaining 3 tablespoons butter. Correct seasonings if necessary. Pour sauce over veal and serve immediately. Serves 8.

WINE: *California Chardonnay or Cabernet Sauvignon*

Veal Riccadonna

12 scaloppine of veal
Seasoned salt and freshly ground black pepper
Flour
2 tablespoons shallots, minced
2 cloves garlic, minced
2 tablespoons butter
3 tablespoons olive oil
½ cup or dry red or white wine
Pinch oregano
1 tablespoon parsley, minced
Pinch cayenne
Juice of 1 lemon

Season the veal on both sides with salt and pepper, then dredge the veal in flour, shaking off any excess.

In a large, heavy skillet, sauté the shallots and garlic in the butter and oil until opaque. Add the veal and sauté 30 seconds on each side, stirring all the while. Pour in the wine to the side, not over the meat. Stir and lift the veal so the wine can flow over and mix well. Add oregano, parsley, cayenne and lemon. Simmer, turning the meat and stirring another minute or so. Put 3 pieces of veal on each of 4 warm plates. Spoon hot sauce over and serve immediately. Serves 4.

WINE: *Mâcon-Villages or Frascati*

Veal Valentino

12 scaloppine of veal
Seasoned salt and freshly ground black pepper
Flour
4 tablespoons butter
½ cup dry sherry
½ cup dry vermouth
½ cup chicken or veal stock
½ cup heavy cream
1–1½ teaspoons tomato paste
½ cup sliced mushrooms
12 cooked asparagus tips

Season the veal and dredge in flour, shaking off the excess. Heat a skillet with 4 tablespoons butter. Sauté the veal over medium heat for 30 seconds on each side. Remove the veal and keep warm. Stir 1–1½ teaspoons flour into the skillet. Cook, stirring, for a minute or so. Still stirring, add the wines, stock and heavy cream. Bring to a light boil, add the tomato paste, lower heat and simmer, stirring, until the liquid has a good consistency. Add the mushrooms and asparagus and correct the seasoning with salt and pepper. Place 3 veal scaloppine on each prewarmed plate. Spoon hot sauce over with mushrooms and asparagus over all. Serve immediately. Serves 4.

WINE: *Carema or Gavi*

Homestyle Veal Stew

2½ pounds veal, cut into 1½-2 inch pieces
5 tablespoons olive oil
1 large red onion, coarsely chopped
4 cups chopped tomatoes (fresh or imported canned)
2 teaspoons chopped fresh basil
Seasoned salt and freshly ground black pepper
2 cloves garlic, crushed in a press
Flour for dredging
1 pound fresh mushrooms, thinly sliced
½ cup dry Marsala wine or sherry
2–2½ cups potatoes, cut into pieces 1½-inches long and ¾-inch thick
2 cups peas (fresh or frozen)
3 tablespoons balsamic vinegar

Heat 1 tablespoon of the oil in a medium skillet, then add the onion and sauté over medium heat until it becomes translucent. Add tomatoes, basil, salt, pepper and garlic. Cover and simmer *gently* for 8–10 minutes.

Salt and pepper the veal and dust with flour. Heat 2 tablespoons olive oil in a large skillet. Quickly sear a few pieces at a time over high heat, turning to brown on all sides. When all the veal is browned, add the mushrooms and Marsala. Lower heat, cover and simmer until the wine is reduced somewhat; add the tomato sauce. Add the potatoes, pepper slightly, cover, and gently simmer for 1 hour. Add the peas and balsamic vinegar and simmer for 5–7 minutes. Correct seasonings and serve with pasta or rice. Serves 8. May also be made with chicken pieces.

WINE: *A red Côtes-du-Rhône or Bourgueil (a Loire wine) or Gattinara*

Stuffed Peppers Napoli

6–8 sweet red peppers (not too large)
½ cup Italian olive oil
1 medium yellow onion, chopped
3–4 links sweet Italian sausage, removed from casings
4–5 cloves garlic, minced
1 28-ounce can imported Italian tomatoes, juice and all
½ cup plus 2 tablespoons red wine
1 teaspoon tomato paste
2–3 tablespoons chopped black olives
3 tablespoons Italian-style bread crumbs
1–2 tablespoons freshly grated Parmesan cheese
3 tablespoons chopped fresh parsley
6 anchovy fillets, drained and chopped
Cayenne pepper
Chicken broth

Using a small, sharp knife, cut around the pepper stems, leaving a small hole. Pull out the cores and use a teaspoon to remove the seeds and ribs.

In a large skillet, heat ¼ of the olive oil. Add the onions and sausage meat and sauté, stirring, until the onion becomes translucent and the sausage is browned, about 2 minutes. Add the garlic and sauté, stirring another minute. Break up the tomatoes and add them to the pan. Add 2 tablespoons wine, tomato paste and olives; cook, stirring until the *liquid* reduces to less than half, about 4–5 minutes. Add bread crumbs, cheese, parsley, anchovies and a good pinch of cayenne. Stuff the peppers with this mixture.

Spread the remaining olive oil in a baking dish just large enough to hold the peppers in a single layer. Add the peppers and place any leftover stuffing on the bottom of the casserole along with ½ cup red wine, and bake in a preheated 350° oven for about 1½ hours, or until the peppers are about to collapse. Serves 6–8.

Note: If the bottom of the casserole seems to be drying out, add a little chicken broth.

WINE: *Chianti or Barolo*

Stuffed Pork Chops with Apples and Pecans

A wonderful wintertime family dish.

6 thick (¾-inch) pork chops, trimmed of fat
Seasoned salt and freshly ground black pepper
Flour
Oil
3 cooking apples, cored, peeled and chopped
1½ cups soft bread crumbs
¾ cup chopped celery
4 tablespoons milk
3 tablespoons soft butter
½ cup chopped pecans
Pinch of sage and allspice

Split pork chops through the center, right to the bone. Season all around and inside with salt and pepper, then dip each chop in flour and brown lightly on both sides.

Mix remaining ingredients with a little salt and pepper added. (A pinch more pepper than usual.) Spread the seasoned stuffing between the split halves of the chops and close them with toothpicks. Put the chops in a baking dish and bake 30 minutes at 350°. Serves 6.

WINE: *Saint-Émilion*

Pork Chops with Artichokes and Tomatoes

4 thick pork chops, trimmed
5 tablespoons fruity Italian olive oil
1 large clove garlic, minced
1 cup skinned and chopped tomatoes, or Italian canned tomatoes
4 artichoke hearts, quartered
4 large brown mushrooms or shiitake, sliced
3 tablespoons dry Marsala or red wine
6 fresh basil leaves, chopped
Seasoned salt and freshly ground black pepper

Heat half the olive oil in a large skillet and add the garlic. Sauté for 1 minute and add the tomatoes, artichokes, mushrooms, wine, basil, salt and pepper to taste. Sauté, stirring, for 2 minutes, then lower the heat and let simmer for about 10 minutes, stirring occasionally.

Meanwhile, brush the chops with the remaining olive oil on both sides and season both sides with the seasoned salt and pepper. Cook under a well-preheated broiler (or charcoal broil) for 6–8 minutes on each side. Transfer to a warm serving platter, pour the sauce over, and serve immediately. Serves 4.

WINE: *Barolo or Rioja*

Pork Chops with Fennel Seeds

4 thick pork chops, trimmed
Seasoned salt and freshly ground black pepper
2 tablespoons olive oil
2 cloves garlic, minced
1 cup Italian canned tomatoes, chopped
Pinch dried red pepper flakes
1 cup dry red wine
1 tablespoon fennel seeds
1 tablespoon chopped parsley

Sprinkle the chops with salt and pepper on both sides. Heat the oil in a large skillet. Add the chops and sauté until browned, about 6–8 minutes per side. Add the garlic and sauté 1 minute, then add the tomatoes, red pepper flakes, wine, fennel and parsley. Lower heat to low position and let simmer for about 20–25 minutes. Serves 4.

WINE: *Chianti or Beaujolais*

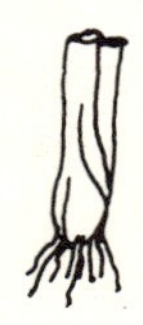

Roast Pork with Orange Sauce

MEAT

1 3½-pound pork loin, bones detached
1½ tablespoons crushed black pepper
2 tablespoons minced rosemary, fresh or dried
4 cloves garlic, minced
1 tablespoon olive oil
Seasoned salt and freshly ground black pepper
½ cup dry red wine
1 cup brown stock, demiglace or mushroom sauce
Grated rind and juice of 1 large orange
2 tablespoons unsalted butter

Preheat oven to 450°. Make 8–10 evenly spaced, shallow (about ⅓ inch) slits over the entire roast.

Combine the pepper, rosemary and garlic. Divide mixture and stuff into the slits in the meat. Brush the roast with olive oil and season with salt and pepper. Place pork in a shallow roasting pan and roast at 450° for 30 minutes. Reduce heat to 325° and cook 1 hour more (or until meat thermometer inserted in the middle of the roast registers 165°). Remove roast to cutting board and let rest.

Discard the grease from the roasting pan. Place pan on top of the stove over medium heat and add the wine, scraping up particles from the bottom of the pan with a wooden spoon. Raise heat to high and let the wine reduce to 2 tablespoons of liquid. Add the stock, orange rind and juice and continue to cook until sauce thickens, stirring all the time (about 4–5 minutes). Lower the heat, whisk in butter. Correct seasoning to taste. Strain into a clean saucepan and keep the sauce warm.

Slice roast and arrange on heated plates. Spoon the sauce over and serve immediately. Serves 6–8.

Note: The pork should be juicy and just past the pink medium-rare stage, never dry. Do not overcook.

WINE: *Chianti*

CHATEAU HAUT-BRION
PREMIER GRAND CRU CLASSE

Flamed Leg of Lamb

1 lean leg of lamb, boned
Seasoned salt and freshly ground black pepper
4 ounces juniper berries, marinated in ½ cup gin for 24 hours
½ cup butter

Season leg of lamb, inside and out, with the salt and pepper. Stuff center part with gin-flavored juniper berries. Reserve gin. Roll and tie lamb with string. Let rest overnight in refrigerator. The gin-soaked berries will tenderize the meat and flavor it subtly.

To cook, brush lamb with butter, roasting in hot oven (450°) for 15 minutes. Turn lamb and baste, reduce heat to 350° and cook approximately another 30 minutes. Keep medium-rare.

To serve, remove string, present whole leg at table and flame with hot juniper-flavored gin. Carve in thin slices and serve each guest with some of the berries. Serves 8–10.

WINE: *A Pauillac*

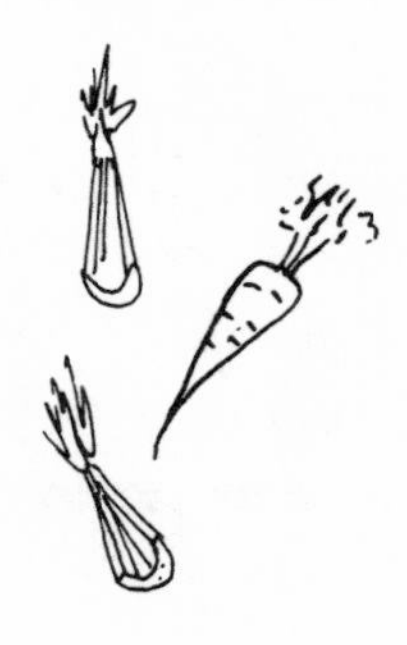

Potato-Tomato Casserole, Sautéed Carrots and Rice Primavera

Grilled Lamb Chops with Jalapeño Mint Jelly

MEAT

4 double-thick lamb chops
Olive oil
1 tablespoon minced garlic
1 tablespoon chopped rosemary
Seasoned salt and freshly ground black pepper
1½ ounces mint jelly
½ jalapeño pepper, minced
1 teaspoon chopped mint
½ teaspoon cider vinegar

Brush lamb chops with olive oil, and sprinkle with garlic and rosemary. Season with salt and pepper. Grill to desired doneness.

Mix rest of ingredients together and spoon over the grilled chops. Serves 2.

WINE: *A red Zinfandel or Barolo*

Noisettes of Lamb Florentine

Noisettes are medallions of lamb cut from the eye of the rack.

8 noisettes of lamb, about 1½ inches thick
2 pounds fresh spinach, stemmed and washed
Seasoned salt
5 tablespoons olive oil
1 clove garlic, minced
Freshly ground black pepper

3 tablespoons unsalted butter
Dijon mustard
3/4 cup dry vermouth
1 cup whipping cream
1/4 cup green peppercorns, rinsed and drained (optional)
1–2 tablespoons chopped parsley for garnish

Combine spinach and a pinch of salt in a heavy saucepan with a cup of water. Bring to a boil, lower heat and let simmer 3 minutes. Transfer to a colander and drain, shaking the colander. Heat 3 tablespoons olive oil in the same saucepan. Add garlic and sauté, shaking, for 1 minute. Add the spinach and sauté, stirring occasionally, for 2 minutes. Season with salt and pepper. Toss and set aside.

Heat 3 tablespoons butter and 2 tablespoons olive oil in a large skillet over medium-high heat until hot. Add the noisettes of lamb (which have already been seasoned with salt and pepper and rubbed gently with Dijon) and cook, turning once, about 4–5 minutes per side for medium-rare. Transfer to heated platter and keep warm.

Discard fat from skillet. Pour vermouth into skillet, stirring and scraping up any browned bits. Boil until liquid is reduced by half. Add cream and peppercorns, slightly cracking or crushing the peppercorns with the back of spoon. Boil until sauce is thickened.

To assemble dish, stir spinach 1 minute over high heat to reheat. Divide spinach evenly on 4 plates. Place the noisettes, 2 on each plate, over the spinach. Top the lamb with the hot sauce and serve immediately. Garnish with a bit of chopped parsley. Serves 4.

WINE: *A spicy Bordeaux: a red Graves or Saint-Estèphe, or Brunello*

Filet Nino

This dish has been a staple at Tony's for years. "Nino" is the Italian equivalent of "Tony."

8 medallions or tournedos of prime tenderloin, about 3 ounces each
Seasoned salt and freshly ground black pepper to taste
½ cup butter
4 large fresh mushroom caps, quartered
8 artichoke hearts, precooked and sliced (frozen or canned)
3 cloves garlic, minced
¼–½ cup good red wine
Chopped parsley

Salt and pepper meat and pan-sauté in butter until half cooked. Then add mushrooms, artichokes, garlic and wine and let simmer to desired degree of doneness. Do not overcook. Serve 2 medallions per guest, with mushrooms, artichokes and sauce spooned over. Garnish with chopped parsley. Serves 4.

WINE: *Gattinara or Chianti*

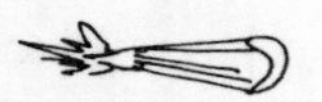

Rump Roast in Barolo Wine

This goes particularly well over wide buttered noodles.

1 3-pound beef rump roast
6 cloves garlic, peeled and thinly sliced
1 bottle Barolo wine or other red wine
2 onions, peeled and chopped

3 carrots, peeled and chopped
3 celery stalks, chopped
3 large tomatoes, sliced
Seasoned salt and freshly ground black pepper
1 bay leaf
1 fresh rosemary sprig or dried rosemary
Pinch of dried thyme
1/4 cup olive oil
1/2 cup balsamic vinegar
1 small glass brandy
Parsley

Pierce meat with a sharp, thin knife and put 1/3 of the garlic slices in roast in various places. Put meat in a large bowl with the wine, vegetables, herbs and spices. Leave to marinate 12 hours, turning occasionally.

Drain the meat thoroughly, reserving the marinade. Heat oil in Dutch oven or roasting pan and brown meat over medium heat, turning, on all sides. Add the reserved marinade, vegetables, herbs and spices and cook over moderate heat for 10 minutes.

Lower heat, cover and simmer gently for 2 hours. Add balsamic vinegar, simmer for 30–45 minutes more, or until meat is tender. Remove meat and keep hot.

Purée the cooking liquid and vegetables in an electric blender or work through a strainer. Return to baking pan, add brandy and bring to a boil for 1 minute.

Slice meat, arrange on a warm serving platter. Pour sauce over and serve immediately. Garnish with chopped fresh parsley. Serves 6–8.

WINE: *A big Barolo*

Sirloin with Porcini and Peppers

MEAT

4 10- to 12-ounce sirloin strips, 1/2- to 3/4-inch thick
1/4 cup unsalted butter
2 cloves garlic, minced
4–5 ounces dried porcini mushrooms
1/2 cup dry Marsala
1/2 cup demiglace or brown stock
2 large red peppers, roasted, peeled, cored and cut into 1/4-inch strips
2 tablespoons olive oil
Seasoned salt and freshly ground black pepper

Soak porcini in water for 15 minutes, rinse 3–4 times and drain thoroughly.

Preheat grill or broiler. In a large heavy skillet, melt 2 tablespoons butter. Over medium-high heat, sauté the garlic until opaque. Add the porcini and toss, sautéing for 1 minute. Remove porcini and garlic and reserve.

Pour out grease, add the Marsala to the same pan, pour in the demiglace and cook over high heat until sauce thickens slightly, 4–5 minutes. Add the garlic and porcini and whisk in the remaining butter. Stir in the roasted pepper strips. Correct seasoning and keep warm.

Meanwhile, brush the steaks on both sides with olive oil and season with salt and pepper on both sides. Grill 2–3 minutes on each side for medium-rare, or broil to desired doneness. Place one steak on each of 4 heated plates and ladle sauce over, equally dividing the peppers and mushrooms over the steaks. Excellent accompaniments are noodles or seasoned wild rice. Serves 4.

WINE: *A red Mercurey or a red Rully or Amarone*

Herbed Paillard of Beef

This is also suitable for fowl or lamb. With lamb, add a little rosemary.

1 2-pound tenderloin
4 tablespoons unsalted butter, softened
5 tablespoons Italian extra virgin olive oil
1 large clove shallot, minced
1 large clove garlic, minced
¼ cup fresh parsley, chopped
Fresh basil to taste
Seasoned salt and freshly ground black pepper
3 tablespoons chopped fresh mint

In a blender or food processor, thoroughly combine butter, 1 tablespoon olive oil, shallot, garlic, parsley, basil, ½ teaspoon seasoned salt and 1 teaspoon freshly ground black pepper. Set aside.

Cut the tenderloin into 4 horizontal slices, each about ¼-inch or less thick (you may have to flatten them slightly). Cut each slice in half.

Have two 14-inch or larger skillets very hot. Put them over high heat for at least 3–5 minutes. When sizzling hot, put 2 tablespoons olive oil in each skillet, immediately followed by half the meat in each skillet. Sear the meat for about 1 minute on each side. Do not overcook! Stir the herb-butter mixture well. Brush it generously on the paillards, sprinkle with chopped mint and serve immediately. Serves 4.

WINE: *Gevrey-Chambertin*

Braised Short Ribs with Red Wine

6 pounds lean short ribs of beef, cut into serving pieces
Seasoned salt and freshly ground black pepper
Flour for dredging
1/3 cup oil
1 large onion, finely chopped
2 carrots, finely chopped
1 stalk celery, finely chopped
1 tomato, finely chopped
2 cloves garlic, finely chopped
1/3 teaspoon savory
1/2 cup beef broth
1 1/2 cups red wine
3 tablespoons balsamic vinegar
1 bay leaf

Preheat oven to 300°. Season ribs well with salt and pepper and dredge in flour. Heat the oil in a large heavy skillet and brown the short ribs on all sides. Over the bottom of a heavy casserole large enough to hold the ribs in one layer, spread all the vegetables and sprinkle the savory over them. Arrange ribs on top.

Heat the broth, wine and vinegar together; crush and sprinkle the bay leaf over the liquid. Pour liquid over ribs. Cover the casserole and place in oven and bake for 3–3 1/2 hours, or until tender. Excellent served with rice or noodles. Serves 6.

WINE: *Red Côtes de Roussillon or Barolo*

Italian-style Steak

4 12-ounce sirloins, T-bones or steak of choice
Seasoned salt and freshly ground black pepper
½ cup Italian extra virgin olive oil
1 teaspoon dried oregano
2 lemon halves
1 tablespoon chopped fresh mint

Preheat grill or broiler to very hot. Season both sides of the steak with seasoned salt and an extra pinch of pepper, and brush with olive oil. Cook steaks 2 minutes per side. Remove steaks, brush again with olive oil and sprinkle with a pinch of oregano and grill or broil for another 3–4 minutes or to desired degree of doneness. Remove steaks, squeeze lemon juice over each, and sprinkle with mint and serve immediately. Excellent with crisp-fried potato slices. Serves 4.

Note: For a variation that should be a command, unless garlic is not your dish: Rub the steak with sliced garlic before cooking.

WINE: *Corvo (Sicilian wine) or Barolo*

Pepper Steak

4 6-ounce filets mignons
Seasoned salt
½ cup very coarse black pepper on a plate
⅓ cup oil
4 tablespoons cognac
⅔ cup demiglace or brown sauce
½ cup heavy cream

Season the filets, top and bottom, with seasoned salt, then press them firmly, top and bottom, in the coarse pepper. Heat the oil in a heavy skillet. When very hot, brown the filets for about 3 minutes on each side. Place steaks on a platter and keep warm in the oven.

Meanwhile, in a saucepan, gently heat the cognac, and when it is very warm, set it ablaze, and pour it flaming over the steaks. When the flame expires, drain the liquid into the sauté skillet with the remaining drippings. Return skillet to moderate heat and stir in the demiglace and cream; heat, but do not boil. Stir well and when the sauce seems the right consistency, pour over the steaks and serve immediately. Excellent served with a well-seasoned wild rice. Serves 4.

WINE: *A red Zinfandel or Cabernet Sauvignon*

Grilled Filet with Stilton Sauce

Tony: "Beef-and-Stilton may sound odd, but they go together superbly to make a remarkable and an unusual dish."

4 filets mignons, 6–8 ounces each
Seasoned salt and freshly ground black pepper
3 tablespoons butter, softened

Sauce:

¾ cup Sercial Madeira
2 tablespoons minced shallots
1 clove garlic, minced
1 cup heavy cream
½ cup demiglace or brown stock
½ cup butter, softened
6 ounces Stilton, Gorgonzola or Bleu cheese, crumbled and softened
Cayenne pepper to taste

Season filets with salt and black pepper and rub all over with softened butter. Grill the filets over charcoal until done. Serve immediately with the sauce and rice or noodles.

For the sauce: In a saucepan, combine the Madeira with the shallots and garlic and reduce the mixture over medium-high heat to about 2 tablespoons. Add the cream and the demiglace or stock and reduce the liquid over high heat to about 1 cup. In a bowl, cream together the butter and the cheese until smooth. Whisk the cheese mixture a little at a time into the saucepan and simmer sauce for 3 minutes. Strain into a serving bowl. Season with cayenne pepper and seasoned salt to taste. Serves 4.

WINE: *A vintage port (a proposal of his that Dewey called, justifiably, "totally revolutionary") or a big Burgundy*

Beef Tenderloin with Morels

8 beef tenderloin slices (2–3 ounces each)
Seasoned salt and freshly ground black pepper
3 tablespoons butter
1 tablespoon finely chopped shallots
2 cloves garlic, finely chopped
2–3 ounces Rainwater Madeira
½-1 teaspoon dry English mustard (½ teaspoon should do, but this should be done to taste)
½ cup demiglace or thick beef gravy
6 ounces morels, cut into quarters
Chopped parsley for garnish

Season beef with the salt and pepper. In a heavy saucepan, over medium-high heat, melt 2 tablespoons butter and sauté the tenderloin slices about 45 seconds to 1 minute on each side, no more. Remove the beef and keep warm.

To the skillet add the remaining butter, shallots and garlic, and sauté, stirring, for 2 minutes. Add the Madeira, mustard, demiglace and morels. Simmer over medium heat for 2–3 minutes. Pour the sauce over the beef and serve at once. Sprinkle chopped parsley over all as a garnish. Serves 4.

WINE: *Pommard*

Calf's Liver Sauté

Devotees of liver will love the effect balsamic vinegar has on this cut of meat.

MEAT

½ pound calf's liver, sliced ¼-inch thick
Seasoned salt and freshly ground black pepper
Flour, well-seasoned with salt and pepper
2 tablespoons butter
1 shallot, minced
3 tablespoons chopped parsley
1 tablespoon balsamic vinegar
1–2 tablespoons red wine

Pat liver dry and season with the salt and pepper lightly. Dredge in the seasoned flour. Heat butter in a heavy skillet over medium-high heat. Add shallot and parsley and stir 1 minute. Add the liver and sauté until firm but still pink, about 1½ minutes per side. Remove liver to warmed plates. Add the vinegar and wine to the pan, scooping up any browned bits. Simmer a few seconds. Pour over the liver and serve immediately. Serves 2.

WINE: *Beaujolais or Côtes-du-Rhône or California Gamay*

Vegetables

Noncooks think it's silly to invest two hours' work
in two minutes' enjoyment; but if cooking is evanescent,
well, so is the ballet.
JULIA CHILD

THE TEXAS COOK BOOK, published in Houston in 1883 by the women of the First Presbyterian Church, was the first cookbook published in Texas. An inspired work, it included a lighthearted recipe from the book's only male contributor. Capt. Joseph C. Hutcheson represented Houston, whose population was around 20,000 in 1883, in the Texas Legislature, where he wrote the bill creating the University of Texas. Though the captain is not known to have been a cook, his recipe proves that he was an inspired writer on food:

To Cook Cornfield Peas

Go to the pea-patch early in the morning and gather the peas, take them home in a split basket. Take them in the left hand and gouge them out with your right thumb until it gets sore, then reverse hands. Look the pea well in the eye to see its color, but cook them anyway, as no color exempts the pea from domestic service, still the grey eye and white lips and cheeks are to be preferred.

Throw the shelled peas mercilessly into hot water and boil them until they "cave in." When you see they are well subdued, take them out and fry them about ten minutes in gravy—a plenty of gravy, good fat meat gravy, and try to induce the gravy to marry and become social with the peas. When you see that the union is complete, so that no man can put them asunder, and would not wish to if he could, put them in a dish and eat them all.

Well, we have changed our minds about cooking vegetables since 1883. But this exemplary early-day Houstonian and Tony Vallone of a century later share a hearty culinary spirit that allows for wit, for imagination and for gustatory adventure.

Tony's family came to America from southern Italy—eggplant country. The pulpy vegetables—tomatoes, zucchini (or summer squash) and above all the eggplant—mark southern Italian cuisine. "Italian cooks," the esteemed Waverley Root has written, "deal with vegetables better than anyone else in the Western world, perhaps because Italian farmers give them better vegetables than anyone else in the Western world."

Rice Primavera

2½ quarts chicken stock

VEGETABLES

8 ounces small zucchini
8 ounces green beans
8 ounces carrots
8 ounces snow peas
4 ounces peas
6 medium mushrooms
12 tablespoons butter (¾ cup)
3 cups arborio Italian rice
½ cup whipping cream
1 cup freshly grated Parmesan cheese
¼ cup finely chopped parsley
Freshly ground black pepper

Bring the stock to a boil in a large saucepan. Lower the heat and keep at a very low simmer.

Trim the ends from zucchini, green beans, carrots and snow peas. Wash and dry vegetables. Slice zucchini and carrots diagonally into ½-inch pieces. Slice green beans and snow peas into 1-inch pieces. Clean and slice the mushrooms.

Melt 8 tablespoons (½ cup) butter in another saucepan and sauté the zucchini, carrots and green beans for 3–4 minutes, tossing frequently. Add snow peas, peas and mushrooms, and sauté for 1 minute. Add rice and cook for 2 minutes, stirring to coat the rice well with butter.

Add 1 cup hot stock to the rice and vegetable mixture. Cook and stir gently for several minutes until the liquid is absorbed. Repeat with 5 more cups of stock, 1 cup at a time, stirring gently all the while until all the liquid is absorbed. When all the stock is absorbed, add the remaining 4 tablespoons butter and cream. Remove from heat and add ⅔ of the Parmesan and parsley. Season with a generous dash of pepper and toss lightly. Sprinkle remaining Parmesan and parsley on top and serve immediately. Serves 6.

Note: Italian rice has a texture different from that of American rice. It should be creamy and, if desired, a dollop of cooked seasoned tomato can go on top of the rice. Red and yellow peppers may also be added for extra color and flavor.

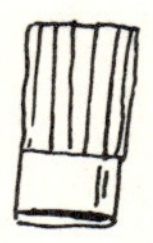

Aunt Mary's Baked Corn

2 heaping cups fresh corn (cut from cob)
2 cups milk
2 tablespoons melted butter
2 tablespoons cornstarch
½ teaspoon black pepper
½-¾ teaspoon seasoned salt
2 eggs, beaten
2 tablespoons sugar
Paprika

First mix well the cornstarch into the milk. When completely dissolved, mix all ingredients together. Pour into a 1½-quart buttered casserole. Sprinkle a little paprika on top for color. Bake in a preheated 375° oven for 1 hour, or until set. Cooking time may vary. Serve immediately. Serves 4–6.

Note: It is very important to scoop the "milk" from the corn cob after cutting the corn. Mix the milk with all the other ingredients.

Italian Vegetable Casserole

A meal in itself.

VEGETABLES

3–4 tablespoons olive oil
1 medium red onion, sliced
3 cups ripe chopped tomatoes
4 tablespoons fresh chopped basil
2 cups chopped eggplant
3 medium potatoes, peeled and cut into thick slices
4 cups green beans, stemmed and cut in half
2 cups zucchini, cut in ½-inch slices
Oregano
Seasoned salt and freshly ground black pepper
2 cups fresh mushrooms, sliced thick
Freshly grated Parmesan cheese
1–2 tablespoons chopped fresh parsley for garnish

Heat the oil in a wide shallow pan. Add onion and sauté. As it takes on color (about 4–5 minutes), add tomatoes and basil. Cover and simmer for 5 minutes, stirring occasionally. Add eggplant, potatoes, beans, zucchini, pinch of oregano, salt and pepper. Cover and cook over moderate heat until potatoes are barely tender. Toss well and add mushrooms and cook 5 more minutes. Transfer to a warm platter, top with another grate or two of pepper, then Parmesan cheese and then chopped parsley. (Any favorite vegetable or combination of vegetables may be added to this dish.) Serves 4–6.

Sautéed Carrots

1 pound carrots, cut into 2-by-½-inch strips, or whole baby carrots
3 tablespoons unsalted butter
½ cup fresh orange juice

Generous pinch of mace to taste
Generous pinch of sugar to taste
Seasoned salt and freshly ground black pepper

In a saucepan of boiling salted water cook the carrots for 3–4 minutes, or until just tender, but on the firm side.

In a small saucepan, melt the butter over moderately high heat, add the carrots, orange juice, mace, sugar, salt and pepper. Cook, stirring until most of the liquid is evaporated and the carrots are somewhat glazed. Serves 4.

Tzimmes

Tzimmes is part of a traditional Passover dinner.

8 large carrots, cut into 1/4-inch slices
1/2-2/3 cup honey
2 tablespoons unsalted butter
1 tablespoon fresh orange juice
Salt

In a saucepan, combine the carrots with enough cold water to cover them by 1 inch and bring the water to a boil over high heat. Simmer the carrots for 4–5 minutes, or until just barely tender. Pour off all the water and add the remaining ingredients with salt to taste. Simmer the carrots for 12–15 minutes, or until they are tender and well coated with the honey mixture. Transfer to warmed serving dish and serve. Serves 6.

Note: During the cooking, you may want to add a squeeze more orange or lemon juice to the honey mixture.

Potato-Tomato Casserole

4 large potatoes
2 tablespoons olive oil
3 large ripe tomatoes, cut into sixths
1½ cups sliced red onion
4 leaves fresh sweet basil, torn into pieces
1½-2 teaspoons seasoned salt
1 teaspoon freshly ground black pepper
3 tablespoons butter
2 tablespoons grated Parmesan cheese

Cut potatoes into eighths. Grease a casserole with olive oil. Put the potatoes, tomatoes, onions, basil, salt and pepper in it. Dot with butter and bake in a 400° preheated oven for 1 hour, or until browned, mixing occasionally. Vegetables will cook down. Sprinkle the grated cheese over all the last 10 minutes of cooking. Serves 4–6.

Braised Leeks, Potatoes and Olives

4 large leeks, roots trimmed, tops cut off, leaving about 2 inches of green part
2 large potatoes, peeled and cut into thirds
1 medium yellow onion, chopped
2–3 tablespoons olive oil
Seasoned salt and freshly ground black pepper
Chicken bouillon
2 tablespoons sliced black olives
1–2 tablespoons chopped parsley for garnish

Preheat oven to 400°. Cut leeks into 2-inch lengths. Place leeks, potatoes, onions, olive oil, salt and a good dash of pepper in casserole with about ¼ inch or so chicken bouillon or broth. Cover and bake for 30–35 minutes. Sprinkle the olives over and bake 5–10 more minutes, or until the leeks are tender. Cooking time will depend on leek size. Garnish with parsley and serve immediately. Serves 4.

Eggplant Nonna

Several years ago Tony cooked this dish with Vic Damone on Dinah Shore's television show. More than 5,000 viewers requested the recipe.

1 large eggplant, cut into ¼-inch slices
½ cup Italian extra virgin olive oil
3–4 cups Spicy Marinara (see page 86)
3 tablespoons chopped fresh or dried basil
1 cup ricotta
1 cup grated Parmesan cheese
½ pound mozzarella cheese, thinly sliced

Heat the oil in a large frying pan over high heat and brown the slices as quickly as possible on both sides. Drain briefly on paper towels. Arrange the slices in a shallow, very lightly oiled baking dish with a little tomato sauce on the bottom of the dish, then eggplant, covering the eggplant with a generous amount of the tomato sauce, chopped basil, ricotta, Parmesan cheese, and lastly, the slices of mozzarella. Place the dish in a hot (450°) oven for about 8 minutes, or until contents are bubbly and the mozzarella is lightly browned. Serves 6.

Note: Eggplant is very watery; to eliminate as much water as possible, raw eggplant slices should be sprinkled with a little salt on both sides and allowed to drain on absorbent towels or on a rack for ½ to 1 hour, pressing slices with a weight. Most of the salt will be washed off as the eggplant drains.

Eggplant Puffs

2 medium eggplants
2 tablespoons seasoned salt
½ cup flour
1 teaspoon seasoned salt
Freshly ground black pepper
3 eggs, well beaten
¼ cup milk
1 cup oil
4 lemon halves

Slice off both ends of eggplants. Do not peel. Cut each eggplant into 1-inch cubes. Put all the cubes in a colander and sprinkle with the 2 tablespoons salt. Toss and let stand for 45 minutes to drain.

Combine the flour, 1 teaspoon seasoned salt and a generous amount of pepper in a plastic bag. Add the eggplant cubes, close the bag and shake it vigorously to coat each piece.

Combine the eggs and milk in a shallow bowl and blend well.

Heat the oil in a large skillet. When hot, but not smoking, dip the eggplant cubes in the egg mixture and put several at a time in the skillet. Leave a small space between each cube. Turn the cubes as they brown and puff on each side (about 2 minutes). Drain on paper towels, squeeze lemon over and serve immediately. Or keep warm in the oven and serve in 15–30 minutes, squeezing the lemon over just before serving. Serves 4–6.

Zucchini with Garlic, Tomato and Basil

4 very large ripe tomatoes
2 pounds medium zucchini
¼ cup Italian extra virgin olive oil
2 teaspoons minced garlic
2 tablespoons minced fresh basil
1 teaspoon seasoned salt
1 teaspoon freshly ground black pepper
1 tablespoon minced fresh parsley

Blanch tomatoes in boiling water for 1 minute. Refresh under cold running water and remove skins. Slice in half lengthwise. Cut the halves into ½-inch cubes. Set aside. Cut ends off the zucchini. Cut zucchini into ½-inch slices.

In a large heavy skillet, heat olive oil over medium heat until hot. Add garlic, turn heat to low and sauté, stirring constantly, until very lightly golden. Add tomatoes and zucchini and cook over medium heat, stirring until zucchini is tender-crisp when tested with a fork, about 5 minutes. Add basil, salt and pepper. Cook 1 more minute. Remove from heat and transfer to a warmed bowl. Garnish with parsley and serve immediately. Serves 6.

Zucchini with Roasted Peppers

1 cup Italian olive oil
3/4 cup thinly sliced red onion
2 pounds small zucchini, washed, trimmed and sliced into 2-by-1/2-inch strips
2 large red sweet peppers, roasted, peeled and thinly sliced
1 teaspoon seasoned salt
1 teaspoon freshly ground black pepper
Basil

In a large skillet, heat olive oil over medium heat until hot. Add onion, turn heat to low and cook, stirring frequently, until soft but not brown, about 4–5 minutes. Add zucchini and cook, stirring frequently, until barely tender when tested with a fork, about 5–6 minutes. Stir in roasted red peppers and continue to cook for an additional minute. Season with salt and pepper. Transfer to a warm bowl. Garnish with fresh basil and serve immediately. Serves 6.

Baked Zucchini

2 pounds medium zucchini
2 extra-large eggs
1 1/2 cups Italian bread crumbs
1/4 cup freshly grated Romano cheese
2 cloves garlic, minced
1 tablespoon chopped fresh parsley
1 tablespoon chopped fresh sweet basil
1/2 teaspoon seasoned salt
1 teaspoon freshly ground black pepper
2–3 tablespoons Italian extra virgin olive oil

Preheat oven to 375°. Brush a large pan with olive oil. Trim off ends of zucchini and cut lengthwise into ¼-inch slices.

In a bowl, beat eggs with a fork. In another shallow bowl, combine all of the remaining ingredients except olive oil. Dip zucchini slices in egg, then dredge on both sides in bread crumb mixture. Arrange slices in a single layer in pan. Drizzle a little olive oil over each slice (you may need a little more olive oil). Bake until slices are lightly golden, about 5 minutes. Remove from oven and turn slices. Continue to bake until slightly crusty and golden, about 7 minutes. Transfer to a warm platter and serve immediately. Serves 6.

Grilled Marinated Zucchini

6 medium zucchini
¾ cup Italian olive oil
2–3 cloves garlic, minced
2–3 tablespoons chopped fresh mint
Seasoned salt and freshly ground black pepper to taste
½ cup red wine vinegar

Cut the zucchini lengthwise into ¼-inch-thick slices. Dip the slices in olive oil and place over a hot grill, preferably a charcoal grill. Grill until marked and turn (about 3–4 minutes in all). Place the grilled zucchini on a serving platter and drizzle the remaining oil over the zucchini (use a little more oil if you want). Combine the garlic and mint and sprinkle over the zucchini. Next, season with salt and pepper to taste. Bring the vinegar to a boil and pour this over the zucchini. Let cool. Cover and marinate in the refrigerator at least overnight. This dish is best when it has been basted and marinated for a couple of days. Serves 4–6.

Fried Zucchini Blossoms

Tony: "Oh, so delicate. At the restaurant, we also stuff and fry them."

20 zucchini or squash blossoms
2 eggs, beaten
Seasoned salt and freshly ground black pepper
Flour for dredging
Oil for frying

Roll the blossoms in the beaten eggs. Add salt and pepper, then dust with flour. Heat about an inch of oil in a medium skillet. When the oil is hot, add blossoms one at a time, just enough to fit comfortably in the pan. Lightly brown them, turning them a few times. Drain on paper towels and serve immediately. A variation is to put a little minced anchovy in each blossom before dipping in egg and flour. Serves 5–6.

Broccoli, Zucchini and Basil Frittata

For lunchtime or a light supper, a perfect main course.

1 pound small firm zucchini
8 ounces broccoli florets
Seasoned salt and freshly ground white pepper
6 tablespoons Italian extra virgin olive oil
3–4 garlic cloves, minced
8 eggs
1/4 cup grated Parmesan cheese
1/4 cup coarsely chopped fresh basil
Pinch of thyme
Pinch of oregano

Trim the ends off the zucchini. Grate the zucchini on large hole of a 4-sided grater. Salt the zucchini, place in a colander and let drain for 30 minutes. Press out the liquid. Heat 3 tablespoons of the olive oil in a large skillet. Add the zucchini, broccoli and garlic and sauté, stirring for 5–6 minutes over high heat. Let cool.

Lightly beat the eggs in a bowl. Add the Parmesan and beat again. Next, add basil, broccoli, zucchini, herbs, salt and a good amount of pepper. Stir to mix well. In a medium nonstick frying pan heat the remaining olive oil. Swirl the oil to coat the pan well, including sides. Add egg mixture and lower heat. Cook slowly, stirring occasionally until the eggs have formed small curds and the frittata is firm, except for the top. To cook the top, place the pan under a hot broiler until the frittata browns lightly. Remove and place a large plate over the skillet and invert the frittata onto it. Serve the frittata with marinara sauce to the side. Any combination of vegetables may be used to make a good frittata. Serves 4.

Fried Artichoke Hearts

1 10-ounce package frozen artichoke hearts
Freshly ground black pepper and seasoned salt
2 eggs, beaten
Flour for dredging
Oil for frying
Lemon wedges

Blanch artichoke hearts in salted water to cover. As soon as water returns to a boil, drain. Grind pepper over the artichokes. Next, sprinkle lightly with seasoned salt. Dip the artichokes in eggs and then dredge in flour. In the meantime, heat 1 inch oil in a small skillet. When oil is hot, add the artichoke hearts, 1 at a time. Fry until crisp and light brown. Blot on paper towels and serve with lemon wedges. Serves 3–4.

Broccoli Rabe and Anchovy Sauce with Orecchiette

Most culinary reference books steer clear of broccoli rabe, but this very Italian vegetable is a bitter-flavored cousin of broccoli with long, thin stalks and leaves resembling those of broccoli. Broccoli rabe, Tony says, does not have the large, tightly closed heads that broccoli does; instead, it has tufts of florets here and there throughout the stalk. "Combined with olive oil, garlic and red peppers," he says, "it is superb. In Italy it is called rappini, and so it is called in many markets here." One diner at Tony's, served rappini for the first time, described it as "charming, perhaps a little more delicate than broccoli."

1 pound broccoli rabe
2¼ tablespoons salt
1 pound orecchiette or similar small pasta
1 can (2 ounces) flat anchovy fillets, drained
5 large cloves garlic, minced
⅓ cup Italian extra virgin olive oil
½ teaspoon freshly ground black pepper
1 cup freshly grated pecorino or Romano cheese

In a large pot, bring 5 quarts water to a full boil over high heat. Wash the broccoli rabe and peel the stems. Cut into 1-inch-long pieces. Add 2 teaspoons of the salt and the broccoli rabe to the boiling water and cook until almost tender, about 2½-3 minutes. Lift the broccoli rabe with a slotted spoon and drain in a colander. Rinse briefly under cold running water.

Let the water in the pot return to a boil. Add the pasta to the boiling water and let cook until *al dente*, about 8–10 minutes.

Meanwhile, mash the anchovies and garlic with a fork. Stir in the olive oil. Scrape the mixture into a large saucepan and cook over low heat until hot (2–3 minutes). Pour the pasta and its water over the broccoli rabe in the colander to reheat it. Drain and add the pasta and broccoli rabe to the saucepan. Season with salt and pepper and toss. Serve immediately with a bowl of the grated cheese to the side. Serve 6–8.

Broccoli, Sunflower Seeds and Mushrooms

This could be called an "Italian stir-fry."

1 large bunch broccoli (2 pounds)
1/4 cup Italian extra virgin olive oil
2 large cloves garlic, sliced in half
12 ounces fresh mushrooms of choice, cleaned and sliced
4–5 tablespoons sunflower seeds, lightly toasted
3/4 teaspoon seasoned salt
1 tablespoon freshly grated Romano cheese

Cut broccoli florets from stems. Wash and drain. Cut florets into bite-sized pieces. Cut off bottoms of stems. Cut them in half horizontally, then slice them into 1½-inch strips.

In a large skillet, heat the oil over a medium flame until hot. Add garlic and sauté, stirring constantly until golden. Discard. Add broccoli stems and sauté, stirring constantly until just barely tender, 4–5 minutes. Add the florets and continue to sauté, stirring all the while, about 3 minutes. Add mushrooms and sunflower seeds and sauté, stirring, about 2 minutes. Season with the salt and a generous dash of the pepper. Transfer to a warmed platter. Sprinkle freshly grated cheese over and serve immediately. Serves 6–8.

Fried Cauliflower

This batter may be used on a variety of vegetables.

1 cup flour
2 tablespoons Italian bread crumbs
Seasoned salt and freshly ground black pepper
2/3 cup dry white vermouth or white wine
2 eggs, beaten
1/2 cauliflower, broken into florets
Oil for frying
Lemon wedges

In a mixing bowl, stir together the flour, bread crumbs, salt, a generous dash of pepper, wine and eggs, then cover and let sit for 1 hour.

Boil cauliflower florets about 5 minutes, then drain. Heat 1 inch oil in a small skillet. When oil is hot, dip the florets one at a time into the batter with tongs, then gently place them in the hot oil and fry, turning occasionally, until they are golden brown. Do not crowd them. Repeat the process, blotting finished florets on paper towels. Serve hot with lemon wedges to the side. Serves 4.

Snow Peas

2 pounds snow peas
3 tablespoons unsalted butter
Seasoned salt and freshly ground black pepper
Allspice
Fresh lemon juice

In a saucepan of boiling water, blanch the snow peas for 10 seconds. Drain them, and refresh them under cold running water and pat them dry.

In a skillet, melt the butter over moderate-high heat, add the peas and toss them until heated through. Season the peas with the salt, pepper and a pinch or two of allspice. Toss them well and transfer to heated serving platter. Sprinkle peas with lemon juice to taste. Toss well and serve immediately. Serves 6.

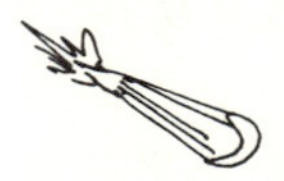

Genoa-style Spinach

An excellent accompaniment to beef, veal, lamb or poultry.

2 pounds fresh spinach, washed, stemmed, cooked and drained
½ cup seedless golden raisins, plumped in white wine and drained
¼ cup toasted pine nuts
Pinch of freshly grated nutmeg
¼ cup Italian extra virgin olive oil
2 tablespoons freshly chopped parsley
4 anchovy fillets, cut into small pieces
Seasoned salt and freshly ground black pepper

Combine spinach, raisins, pine nuts and nutmeg in medium bowl. Heat olive oil in large saucepan over medium heat. Add parsley and anchovies. Reduce heat to low and stir until anchovies are reduced to paste. Stir in spinach mixture, cover and cook over low heat 3–4 minutes. Season with salt and pepper and serve immediately. Serves 4–6.

Spinach with Raisins and Pine Nuts

This is a popular side dish in Rome.

3 pounds fresh spinach
1/3 cup seedless white raisins
6 tablespoons Italian extra virgin olive oil
2 cloves garlic, finely minced
1/2 teaspoon salt
1/3 cup pine nuts, prebrowned lightly in oven

Soak the raisins in warm water for 10 minutes. Drain. Remove any tough stalks from the spinach (you must use fresh spinach), wash briskly and thoroughly, then drain briefly. Cook in the water that clings to its leaves in a covered saucepan on moderate-high heat until the leaves are tender (about 2–3 minutes). Drain, cool and pat dry.

In a large heavy skillet, heat the olive oil over moderate-high heat. Add the garlic and just as soon as it begins to turn opaque add the spinach and cook, stirring and tossing with a fork for 1 minute. Add salt, pine nuts and raisins (drained). Correct seasonings and cook, stirring with a fork for 3 minutes. Serve immediately. Serves 6.

Sautéed Dandelion

Dandelion, or *cicoria* as the Italians call it, makes a wonderful hot green vegetable or a slightly bitter salad. "Served cold as a salad with vinaigrette and goat cheese, it's phenomenal," says Tony.

5 tablespoons olive oil
3 cloves garlic, minced

Crushed red pepper flakes, to taste
2½ pounds fresh dandelion greens
Seasoned salt

Wash and boil greens for about 20 minutes; drain.

Heat the oil in a large skillet, then add garlic and pepper flakes. As garlic begins to turn opaque, add boiled and drained dandelion greens. Season with salt to taste. Cover and lower heat and cook about 5 minutes, tossing often. A squeeze or two of lemon before serving is a nice option. Serves 6.

Escarole Sauté

Tony: "Escarole, one of my favorite greens, is easy to prepare, inexpensive and lends itself to many dishes."

1 large head escarole
2 cloves garlic, minced
4–5 tablespoons Italian olive oil
Seasoned salt
Freshly ground black pepper

Remove outer leaves of escarole. Separate escarole well. Wash thoroughly. Cut leaves in half. Heat olive oil in a skillet and sauté garlic until opaque. Add the escarole and cook over a medium-low flame, stirring all the time for about 4–6 minutes, or until tender. Salt and pepper to taste and serve immediately. Serves 4.

Stuffed Escarole

½ pound chopped or ground lean beef
5 tablespoons Italian extra virgin olive oil
1 tablespoon pine nuts, lightly browned
2 cloves garlic, chopped
1 tablespoon white raisins, chopped
5 ripe olives, chopped
1 tablespoon grated Parmesan cheese
½ cup Italian-style bread crumbs
4 anchovy fillets, chopped
1 tablespoon chopped fresh parsley
Seasoned salt and freshly ground black pepper to taste
2 medium heads escarole

Fry beef in 2 tablespoons olive oil until slightly browned. Remove from fire. Add nuts, garlic, raisins, olives, cheese, bread crumbs, anchovies, parsley, a pinch of salt and a generous dash of the pepper. Mix thoroughly. If too dry, add a few drops of water and a few drops of olive oil until consistency seems slightly moist and right.

Remove a few outer leaves from escarole and discard. Wash escarole well, open from center and flatten out leaves. Place half the mixture in the center of the escarole. Close leaves around the stuffing and tie with white twine so the stuffing does not fall out. Arrange escarole in a pan and pour the balance of the olive oil over all. Cover tightly and cook over low flame for about 20 minutes, or until the escarole is tender. Turn occasionally to prevent burning. If needed, add more olive oil and a tablespoon of water. Wonderful as an appetizer, side dish or main course. Serves 4.

Desserts

Never eat more than you can lift.

MISS PIGGY

One does not age at the table.

ITALIAN PROVERB

HERE IS THE CHAPTER for those who always remember to "leave room for dessert," especially for those—and hang what people think!—indulgent enough to eat *two*. As Gerald Nachman once wrote in scorn of dieters and fitness addicts, "If you're not going to eat dessert, there is little reason to sit down in the first place. I'm willing to plow through almost any meal if there's even a small chance that the dessert will make it worthwhile."

Nachman's zeal is a poor thing compared to that of a Texas woman whose dessert priority was more straightforward. Much more. Her niece, observing Tony's dessert cart with stoic discipline one day, was moved to tell of her late aunt's selfless devotion to desserts. Visiting at the niece's home in Galveston when the niece was a girl, the aunt would ask to be served her dessert at the start of the meal. "You're such a good cook," she would tell her sister, the niece's mother, "that I might not have room for the best part if I have dinner before the dessert."

Nachman should sit down at Tony's, famous for its desserts, especially famous for soufflés, of which James Street was inspired to write, with an estimable pun, that "surely frivolity can rise to no greater height!" For all that, it may be with chocolate—the black, the brown and the white—that Tony's desserts fulfill their culinary destiny. One woman has long vexed her husband because she is so frugal, so fitness-minded, in ordering a meal at Tony's, "so I can feel free to be a lush for something stronger then booze—Tony's chocolate desserts."

Though not chocolate, one of the restaurant's striking desserts—really an architectural creation—is the Raspberry Vacherin (photo opposite page 250), with its countless white meringue fingers extending from the dessert's surface. It has been compared to a lady's hat of the 1890s and to a bristling porcupine in a great snowstorm. As a young man said upon ordering the dessert one day, "I'll have a piece of the cake with the French fries on it." Carol Andrews, the hostess one night, overheard one woman say to another as two couples left the restaurant: "I always feel that I should go to confession after eating one of Tony's desserts."

Most of the wines the panel has recommended throughout the book are moderately priced, but nearly all dessert wines are expensive. Among them are Barsac, Gewürztraminer, Sauternes, Tokay and Trockenbeerenauslese. Add to those Italy's Picolit, sometimes called Italy's Château d'Yquem, port and cream sherry and you have the traditional dessert choices.

Two dessert wines that are less expensive than those come from California's Quady Winery: Essensia and Elysium. They are worthwhile, thriftier alternatives.

Many of the desserts featured in this chapter are the creations of Mercedes Dewey, Tony's pastry chef *par excellence*. Others are simple favorites from the Vallone family.

Biscottini

3 large eggs
3/4 cup sugar
1/2 cup butter
3 cups flour
2 1/2 teaspoons baking powder
1/2 teaspoon salt
1 tablespoon anisette liqueur or oil of anise
1 1/4 cups ground almonds

Cream first 3 ingredients together. Add flour, baking powder and salt after sifting together. Add anisette and almonds, kneading the mixture to blend. Divide dough into 3 parts and shape into rolls about the thickness of your wrist. Bake in 350° preheated oven on cookie sheet 30 minutes. Remove and cut at angles into 1/2-inch slices. Bake 15 minutes longer until firm. Put in airtight tin. These improve with age.

Peach Fool

4 large, very ripe peaches, peeled, pitted and quartered
3 tablespoons powdered sugar
1 tablespoon lemon juice
½ teaspoon cinnamon
1 cup chilled heavy cream
Few drops vanilla

In a food processor or blender, purée the peaches with 1 tablepoon sugar, the lemon juice and the cinnamon until smooth. Transfer the mixture to a bowl and chill it, covered, in the refrigerator for at least 2 hours.

In a chilled bowl, beat the cream with the vanilla and 2 tablespoons of the sugar until it holds soft peaks. Fold it into the purée and divide the dessert into prechilled bowls or dessert glasses. Garnish with some extra peeled, sliced peaches or with nuts or mints, or whatever you desire.

Note: If you make a lot and have some left over, freeze it. It makes a very tasty frozen snack also.

Berry Velvet

This dessert is very simple and has many variations such as the addition of sherbets, liqueurs or other fruits and berries.

2 cups strawberries, raspberries, or other fresh fruit
2 medium bananas
½ cup fresh orange or other juice

Rinse and hull the berries and place them in a plastic bag. Cut the bananas into 1-inch chunks and immediately roll tightly in plastic wrap. Place the fruits in the freezer and freeze solid.

At serving time, place the frozen fruits in the container of a food processor, pour in the juice and process with the metal blade. Blend until the fruit becomes amalgamated into a creamy pink mass. Serve at once while the mixture is still thick. Beautiful in pretty wine glasses. Serve before it melts and do not overprocess. Garnish as desired. Serves 6.

Oranges in Vodka

A refreshing light dessert; one Tony's diner was overheard to describe it as "a screwdriver with texture."

4 oranges
6 tablespoons vodka, or to taste
4–6 tablespoons sugar
Chopped fresh mint

Peel oranges and cut crosswise into ⅓-inch slices. Remove seeds. Arrange slices in a single layer on a plate. Sprinkle vodka and sugar over them and chill for 2–3 hours. Just before serving, arrange slices on 4 chilled salad plates, sprinkle juices over them and fresh chopped mint. This may also be served with a small scoop of orange ice or sherbet in the middle of the dish. Serves 4.

Baked Pears

8 pears
16 whole cloves
2 tablespoons fresh lemon juice
1 lemon, cut in half
2½ cups sugar
3 cups champagne
2 cups water
2 tablespoons Cointreau or other orange-flavored liqueur
2 grated orange rinds
2 cinnamon sticks
Fresh mint

Peel the pears, leaving the stems intact. Stud each pear with a clove near the top and bottom. Immediately drop the pears into a bowl of cold water containing the juice of 1 lemon and the lemon halves.

In a saucepan, combine the sugar, champagne, water, orange liqueur, orange rind and cinnamon sticks. Bring the liquid to a boil over moderate heat, stirring to dissolve the sugar. Put the pears in a casserole large enough to hold the pears in one layer. Pour syrup over them. Bake at 350°, covered, turning them once, for 25 minutes, or until just tender. Cooking time will vary according to pears. Let the pears cool in the syrup. Serve them well-chilled with some of the syrup spooned over and garnished with fresh mint leaves. Serves 8.

Raspberry Gelato

5 pints red raspberries
1 pint heavy cream
1 pint half-and-half
1 cup sugar

Purée raspberries and strain to remove seeds. Mix together purée, cream, half-and-half and sugar to taste. Freeze in an ice-cream machine according to manufacturer's instructions. Or freeze in trays until very firm around edges, then beat with electric mixer until fluffy; refreeze. Makes about ½ gallon.

Zabaglione

6 egg yolks
3 tablespoons sugar
½ cup sweet Marsala

Combine egg yolks and sugar in a double boiler over simmering water, whisking constantly until texture is creamy and color is a pale yellow. Incorporate Marsala in a thin stream while keeping up the beating 8–10 minutes. When finished, the mixture is thick and about the consistency of mayonnaise.

Serve over cold fresh figs or peaches.

Broiled Pineapple

1 3½-pound pineapple
¼ cup unsalted butter, melted
2 tablespoons Kirschwasser (cherry liqueur)
Powdered sugar
Cinnamon
Brown sugar

Peel, core and cut the pineapple into ½-inch rings. Pat the rings dry. Arrange the rings in a buttered casserole in 1 layer. In a small bowl, mix the butter and the Kirschwasser and brush pineapple with the mixture. Next, sprinkle the pineapple with a little powdered sugar, then sprinkle with cinnamon to taste and top this with a light sprinkling of brown sugar. Under a preheated-to-hot broiler, cook the pineapple about 4 inches from heat for 2–3 minutes, or until bubbly. Serve immediately on warmed dessert plates and garnish with a dollop of *crème fraîche*, sour cream or whipped cream. Serves 8.

Chilled Zabaglione with Raspberries

4 large egg yolks
½ cup powdered sugar
Pinch of salt
½ cup sweet Marsala or *½ cup framboise raspberry liqueur* or *¼ cup Marsala and ¼ cup framboise*
⅓ cup heavy cream
24 fresh raspberries

In a metal bowl set over simmering water, combine the egg yolks, sugar and salt and whisk rapidly or use an electric mixer and beat for about 5 minutes, or until thick and fluffy. Add the Marsala in a thin stream, beating constantly, and continue to beat another 6–8 minutes, or until the mixture is about triple in volume, holds soft peaks and feels warm to the touch.

Transfer the mixture to a bowl set in a bowl of cracked ice and stir until cold. In a small, chilled bowl, beat the cream until it holds stiff peaks and fold it into the chilled mixture along with the fresh raspberries, saving 1 to top each zabaglione. Spoon the zabaglione into individual dessert glasses, top each with a raspberry and chill for at least 1 hour.

Once you get it down, zabaglione are easy to make, lend themselves to endless variations and are always popular. Serves 4.

Marie Antoinette Pudding

2 cups heavy cream
½ cup sugar
¼ teaspoon salt
2 tablespoons melted butter
1 teaspoon grated lemon rind
½ teaspoon grated orange rind
4 beaten egg yolks
2 cups cubed pound cake or similar yellow cake
1 cup white raisins, soaked in ½ cup bourbon
½ cup blanched, sliced almonds

Scald the cream. Mix separately the sugar, salt, butter, lemon rind and orange rind. Pour cream and sugar mixture over beaten egg yolks and mix until well blended.

Add the cake cubes, raisins and almonds and blend lightly.

Place ingredients in buttered baking dish. Place dish in a pan and pour water into the pan to a depth of 1 inch. Bake at 325° for 1 hour. Cool and serve with *crème anglaise* flavored with bourbon.

Sicilian Cassata

9-inch pound cake
1 pound ricotta
2½ tablespoons heavy cream
½ cup sugar
4 tablespoons Cointreau or other orange liqueur
4 tablespoons candied fruit, chopped
3 tablespoons semisweet chocolate pieces
Chocolate frosting

Slice the end crusts and the top off of the pound cake. Cut cake lengthwise into ¾-inch slices.

Put ricotta through coarse sieve or food mill, then beat in mixer until smooth. While beating, add heavy cream, sugar and orange liqueur. Incorporate candied fruit and chocolate pieces.

Spread above mixture on bottom slice of pound cake. Place second layer on first. Repeat process until all slices are used. Refrigerate until mixture is firm (about 1 hour).

Cover and decorate with your favorite chocolate frosting.

Monte Bianco

1 cup heavy cream
6 tablespoons sugar
2 tablespoons rum
1 16-ounce can chestnut purée
Additional cup heavy cream, whipped

Whip 1 cup heavy cream with sugar, add rum and incorporate into chestnut purée. Put mixture through a potato ricer and form into a cone shaped to a peak. Decorate with more whipped cream (sweetened, if desired) to resemble a mountain of snow.

Concorde

Meringues:

6 egg whites
3/4 cup sugar
4 tablespoons cocoa powder
1 cup powdered sugar

Mousse:

6 ounces semisweet chocolate
7 tablespoons butter
3 egg yolks
5 egg whites
5 1/2 teaspoons sugar

Prepare meringues: Set oven to 250°. Take baking sheet and cover with buttered wax paper. Beat egg whites until they are firm, gradually adding 1/3 of the sugar as you do this. When egg whites are firm, add remaining 2/3 of the sugar slowly.

Mix cocoa powder with powdered sugar. Fold into egg whites.

Draw 3 circles about 8 inches in diameter on wax paper. Fill circles with meringue, using spatula.

Make long meringue strips using pastry bag and placing on wax paper on a cookie sheet, using number 3 piping tip.

Bake circles in 250° oven 2 hours. Bake strips in 250° oven until firm to the touch, about 45 minutes–1 hour. Allow meringues to cool.

Make chocolate mousse: Melt chocolate in double boiler, add butter, stir, cool. Stir in egg yolks slowly. Beat egg whites until stiff, then add sugar and beat awhile longer. Fold chocolate into egg whites. Blend well. Cool.

Assembly: Place 1 round meringue on serving plate. Spread with mousse. Top with second meringue, repeat process. Cover with third meringue, completely cover with mousse on top and sides. Cut up long meringue strips into small pieces. Use to decorate cake; sprinkle with powdered sugar.

Bocconate

1 large egg yolk
4 tablespoons sugar
1 tablespoon all-purpose flour
¼ teaspoon vanilla
½-¾ teaspoon lemon peel
½ cup cold milk
1 cup unsifted all-purpose flour
2 teaspoons sugar
Dash of salt
1 tablespoon olive oil
¼ cup sweet white wine
Raspberry preserves
1 egg, beaten with 1 tablespoon milk
Powdered sugar

Blend egg yolk, sugar and 1 tablespoon flour in the top of a double boiler. Add vanilla and lemon peel, stir in milk and cook over medium heat, stirring constantly, until thickened and smooth. Do not allow to boil. Cover and chill.

Combine 1 cup flour, sugar and salt. Place in a mound on a nonstick surface and make a well in the center. Add oil and wine and blend until smooth. Knead well. On a lightly greased surface, roll out half of the dough to ⅛-inch thickness. Spoon teaspoonfuls of cold custard 4 inches apart on dough. Top the custard with small dollop of preserves.

Roll out remaining dough and place over custard filling. Press down around filling and cut into squares with a pastry wheel. Brush each square with egg mixture and arrange on greased baking sheets.

Bake at 375° for 20 minutes or until golden. Serve warm, if desired, sprinkled with powdered sugar.

Tiramisu

Extremely popular at the restaurant, this rich custard dessert is easy to make at home. The secret: Mascarpone cheese, a triple-cream cheese. Ordinary cream cheese will not work in this recipe. *Tiramisu* literally means "pick me up" in Italian, a reference to its caffeine content.

3 egg yolks
1/4 cup powdered sugar
2 tablespoons rum
1 pound Mascarpone cheese
1/2 cup strong espresso
1/4 cup Tía María
9 lady fingers (must be good-quality)
Sweetened whipped cream
Sweet chocolate shavings

Whisk the yolks with sugar and rum until light. Add the Mascarpone, which has been allowed to soften briefly outside the refrigerator (it sours quickly if left at room temperature for too long a time). Beat the cheese into the egg-sugar mixture until smooth.

Spoon some of this mixture into a 9-inch quiche pan or pie plate. Dip the lady fingers into a mixture of the espresso and Tía María. Arrange the moistened lady fingers on the Mascarpone mixture. Spoon the remaining cheese mixture on the lady fingers.

Cover the dish with plastic wrap and refrigerate overnight. Before serving, decorate with whipped cream and chocolate shavings.

Mocha Log

13 whole eggs
2 cups sugar
2 cups flour
3/4 cup cornstarch
Sweetened whipped cream
Chocolate curls

Genoise: Break 13 whole eggs in a bowl. Add 2 cups sugar. Whisk together in the top of a double boiler until mixture reaches room temperature. Transfer to mixer and beat until it triples in size.

Mix 2 cups flour and 3/4 cup cornstarch in a mixer at minimum speed. Blend flour and cornstarch into egg mixture a little at a time, being careful mixture does not deflate.

Line two cookie sheets with buttered wax paper or parchment. Dust lightly with flour. Spread batter carefully and evenly over the cookie sheets. Bake in 350° oven for 10 minutes.

Invert genoise layers onto two fresh sheets of wax paper that have been sprinkled with powdered sugar. Peel away baking papers from the genoise layers and sprinkle layers with powdered sugar while they are still warm. Allow to cool.

Line the inside of a 12-inch loaf pan with wax paper, cutting away excess paper at corners. Use this liner as a pattern to cut one of the genoise layers into a shape that will fit into the loaf pan as a liner. Return your paper liner to the pan, then carefully line the pan with the pre-cut genoise.

Fill the center of the loaf with Mocha Mousse (see page 251), and cut a rectangle from the remaining genoise layer to cover the top of the loaf. Refrigerate overnight. Unmold onto serving dish and decorate with sweetened whipped cream and chocolate curls.

The dessert cart's Raspberry Vacherin (recipe not included), Berry Velvet and a serving of the Concorde

Sous Chef
Bobby

Mocha Mousse

2 envelopes unflavored gelatin
1½ cups espresso (made very strong)
4 egg whites at room temperature
¼ teaspoon cream of tartar
¾ cup sugar
1⅓ cups chilled, whipped heavy cream
⅓ cup Captain Morgan's spiced rum
¾ teaspoon vanilla
½ square semisweet chocolate in shavings

Sprinkle gelatin over the 1½ cups of espresso at room temperature; dissolve, stirring over low heat; cool.

Beat the egg whites until foamy. Add the cream of tartar, and beat, adding sugar by the spoonful until stiff. Place bowl of whipped cream in a pan containing several inches of ice and water.

Add the rum and vanilla to coffee-gelatin mixture, stirring well. Fold half of the coffee mixture into the egg whites. Fold this into the whipped cream. Fold remaining coffee-gelatin mixture into cream-egg white mixture. Refrigerate. After 6–7 minutes, lightly fold over the contents of the bowl with a spatula.

Leave in the refrigerator and check after about 10 minutes. Fold over again lightly with a spatula if not blended well. Do not let the mixture separate into 2 layers; keep checking and folding over if necessary. You may have to fold over 2 or 3 times. As soon as the mousse is almost set, spoon it lightly into the desired serving dish or bowl, which has been prechilled. Sprinkle with the grated chocolate as a garnish.

Chef Robert Vasquez removes dessert soufflés from oven.

Spumoni Cheesecake

Almond layer:

4 tablespoons blanched almonds
3 tablespoons whipping cream
1/4 teaspoon almond extract
11 ounces cream cheese, cut into small pieces
2 eggs
2/3 cup sugar
Few drops green food coloring
1/4 cup Amaretto liqueur

Mix first 3 ingredients in food processor until smooth. Add other ingredients, processing again until smooth.

Cherry layer:

11 ounces cream cheese
2 eggs
2/3 cup sugar
10 ounces sour cherry preserves
1 jigger Cherry Heering

Mix all ingredients until smooth.

Apricot layer:
Same as cherry layer, except substitute 3/4 cup dried, finely chopped apricots for cherries and apricot liqueur for Cherry Heering.

Crust:

1/2 cup all-purpose flour
1/4 cup well-chilled butter, cut into small pieces
3 tablespoons sugar

For the crust, preheat oven to 325°. Butter bottom of a 9-inch springform pan. Blend flour, butter and sugar until mixture holds together. Press evenly into bottom of pan. Bake until golden brown, about 15 minutes.

When crust is ready, place almond mixture in the springform. Bake until center no longer moves when shaken, about 20 minutes. Repeat process with each mixture by stages: bake first layer, then when ready, fill with second layer. Bake, then go on to the third. Decorate with sweetened whipped cream, almonds and cherries.

Lemon Mousse

1 cup sugar
5 jumbo eggs
½ cup unsalted butter, melted
Juice of 5 lemons
1½ tablespoons lemon zest
2 cups heavy cream, whipped

Beat sugar and eggs about 5½ minutes with electric mixer. Add melted butter a little at a time while mixer is on. Incorporate lemon juice and zest. Pour mixture into a double boiler. Cook over low heat about 15 minutes, whisking as you do so.

Transfer to bowl and refrigerate about 1½ hours. Stir a couple of times during refrigeration. When cool, incorporate whipped cream and divide into individual serving bowls or demitasse cups. Garnish as desired.

Tony's Apple Tart

Crust (makes 1 shell):

1½ cups flour
½ cup unsalted butter, cut in small pieces
¾ teaspoon sugar
⅛ teaspoon salt
About ¼ cup cold water

Mix flour with butter, sugar and salt. (Use hands to mix butter into flour.) When finished, you must see bits of butter in the dough. Add water and continue kneading until ingredients hold together. Refrigerate.

Filling:

3½ pounds good cooking apples
1 cup sugar
½ cup unsalted butter
1 cup water

Roll out dough, cut out a 9-inch circle and place on a cookie sheet. Puncture dough liberally with fork. Bake, unfilled, in a 400° oven for 10 minutes. Cool. Slide onto serving plate.

Trim, peel and slice apples. Mix sugar and butter in a heavy skillet until syrup is formed. Sauté apples in syrup 5–6 minutes. When soft, pour onto large cookie sheet to cool. When cool, arrange slices on tart shell. Cover with the leftover caramel syrup. Serve immediately. Serves 8.

Apricot Soufflé

½ pound dried apricots
2½ cups boiling water
¾ cup sugar
6 eggs
2 egg whites
½ cup heavy cream
1 tablespoon Kirsch
1 tablespoon orange liqueur
Juice of ½ lemon
11 ounces cream cheese, softened
1 tablespoon butter
Powdered sugar

Put the apricots in a small pot. Pour the boiling water over, cover, and put aside for 1 hour. Stir in the sugar, bring to a simmer and cook uncovered for 20 minutes. Cool for 20 minutes. Preheat the oven to 375°. Break the eggs into a blender or food processor. Add the extra egg whites, cream, Kirsch, orange liqueur and lemon juice. Process or blend. Add the cooked apricots and process mixture to purée the fruit.

Finally, add the cream cheese, breaking it into chunks as you add it. Thoroughly incorporate each chunk of cream cheese before you add another one. Give a final burst at high speed.

Butter a 6-cup soufflé mold. Pour in the batter to about the ¾ level or a little higher; do not fill to the top. Bake for about 50–55 minutes or until the top is lightly browned and a little puffy. Sprinkle powdered sugar over and serve at once. Serves 4–6.

Note: This should produce a soufflé that is still soft in the center. The slightly custardy center serves as a sauce to spoon over the rest of the soufflé. If you want, you can bake the soufflé longer and make your own sauce to serve with it.

Vanilla Soufflé

This is the base for most dessert soufflés.

2 tablespoons butter
1½ tablespoons flour
½ cup scalded milk
1 vanilla bean or *⅓ teaspoon vanilla*
5 egg yolks
5 tablespoons sugar
6–7 egg whites
Pinch of cream of tartar
Powdered sugar

Melt 2 tablespoons butter in a skillet and add 1½ tablespoons flour and cook, stirring constantly until the mixture just starts to turn golden. Add the scalded milk and the vanilla bean (or add ⅓ teaspoon vanilla extract after the mixture has cooked). Cook the sauce over medium-low heat, stirring constantly until the sauce has thickened, and then continue cooking, stirring, for 5 minutes more. Remove the vanilla bean or add the extract.

Beat 5 egg yolks well with 4 tablespoons sugar and combine them with the batter. Beat the egg whites with a pinch of cream of tartar until stiff, adding 1 tablespoon sugar during the last minute of beating. Fold them into the batter. Do not mix the batter and egg whites well. Pour the batter into a buttered, lightly sugared soufflé dish and bake the soufflé in a 400° oven for about 20 minutes, or until it is well puffed and delicately browned. Sprinkle powdered sugar on top and serve immediately. Serves 4–6.

CHOCOLATE SOUFFLÉ:

Follow recipe for vanilla soufflé and in the hot milk melt 2 squares of grated semisweet chocolate. To this mixture add 1 more tablespoon sugar.

COFFEE SOUFFLÉ:

Follow recipe for vanilla soufflé and to the base add 2 tablespoons espresso or strong coffee.

RASPBERRY SOUFFLÉ:

Flavor 1 cup crushed fresh or frozen raspberries with 1 tablespoon framboise (raspberry liqueur) and 2 tablespoons sugar. Follow the vanilla soufflé recipe and add the berries to the thickened base. Serve with a sauce made up of coarsely chopped raspberries and framboise-flavored sweetened whipped cream.

HALF-AND-HALF SOUFFLÉ:

Follow the recipe for vanilla soufflé and pour ⅔ of the batter into a buttered and sugared soufflé mold. Make a shallow depression in the batter. Carefully fold into the rest of the batter 2 tablespoons melted semisweet chocolate. Pour the chocolate batter into the center of the vanilla batter, leaving a rim of vanilla. Lightly smooth the soufflé with a spatula. Bake as usual (it may take 5 or 6 minutes longer). The chocolate and vanilla mixtures will remain separate.

Index

DESIGN: Whitehead & Whitehead
TYPESETTING: G & S Typesetters
TYPE: Galliard *with* Cochin
PRINTING: Hart Graphics
BINDING: Ellis Bindery
1986